TRI- STATE
TRIANGLE

Hu$tle with Fine$$e

Presents :

TRI- STATE
TRIANGLE

An Urban Fiction Novel

by

Tamika D. Harding

Library of Congress Control Number:2009931126

ISBN:0-615-27239-8

CoverDesign/Graphics:Jamar Hargrove/Matt Pramshufer

Author:TamikaD.Harding

Editor-In-Chief: Tamika D. Harding

Printed in the United States of America

CONTENTS

DEDICATED TO
LELIA BRANDON

SUNRISE

January 16, 1918

SUNSET

November 16, 2006

You were the one who said that "I would grow up to be something special" when I was just a young child. May you rest in peace grand mom I'm going to make you proud and make the whole world see what you saw in me.

&
Peter & Marlene Harding

Even though we don't always see eye to eye I still love the both of you very much. God Bless the both of you.

About the Author

My name is Tamika D. Harding I was born on September 1, 1977 in Chester, Pennsylvania. I graduated from Chester High School in 1995. Since my graduation I've been trying to find my way through life working different jobs until I found a few of my hidden talents and pursued a career in music as a Rapper. Being the business minded woman that I am I tried to start a record label in the process. After a few years had passed and still not being successfu at my music career I decided to try something else. Now I'm currently starting a publishing company deciding to choose a career as a successful Author and business woman. Later I intend to start a clothing line, open a chain of restaurants, film movies, and eventually get back to starting a Record label. You can expect to read a lot more books from me as I strive to be the best at whatever I do.

ACKNOWLEDGEMENTS

First of all I would like to thank the all mighty God without him blessing me with the gift of creativity this wouldn't be possible. I would like to thank my brother (Marvin) and my sister (Kim) for always giving me some encouraging words when I'm feeling down and just about to give up. I would like to thank my nieces (Lakeisha & Regina) for always putting a smile on my face when I need it. I would like to thank my nephew (Winston) for being such a pain in the butt (Laff out Loud). As for the rest of my family I forgive you all for you know what and even though we are not a close knit family I love all of you as if we were. I would like to thank Lakia Mason and April Allen for giving me motivation to finish this book and for giving me direction on getting this out to the public. I would like to thank Devon "Feet" Potts for telling me to "Reach for the stars". I also would like to thank Saniyyah Dodson for telling me in so many words "get back on your job" when I lost my focus and even though you hate my guts I still got love for you. I also would like to thank all of the people who ever smiled in my face then talked about me behind my back, never wanted to see me succeed through life, don't like me for whatever reason, treated me wrong, called me names or any other disrespect, because of your negative energy I continue to grow, achieve my goals and make a way out of thin air, you make me better by putting fire under my feet with that negative energy so thank you very much. I want to give a shout to the Chester High School Class of 1995 "If you fail to plan you plan to fail." If that wasn't some true shit they told us at graduation Laff out Loud, see you all at the reunion next year. Dueces. Last but not least I would like to thank Porsche who has been nothing but supportive since the day we met, thanks for motivating me to finish what I started. If there is anyone else I forgot to mention after all this writing I did to complete this book my bad I'll get you on the next one.

LETTER TO MY READERS,

I would like to thank you all for supporting my first book by making this purchase. I hope to gain all of you as fans of my work. This is only the beginning ladies and gentlemen. So please look for future projects from me real soon. I had a lot of fun writing this book and found the author inside of myself so I hope you like it.

I would like to say that in no way is this a true story. I used the Tri State area as my stage to create this story. I hope you enjoy yourself as much as I did because you are about to go on an adventure ride so buckle up.

CHAPTER ONE:

THE BOSS

Tamia took a long pull of her Dutch Master then exhaled.

"I have to get my life right, I can't keep doing the things that I'm doing I'm getting too old for this shit". She thought to herself as she pulled up in front of Bourbon's house.

She was already outside with 2cent and Redds.

"What's good cousin why don't you take this ride with me". Tamia said after she rolled down the window.

"Alright" Redds and 2cent said in unison. Bourbon hopped in the front seat as Redds and 2cent hopped in the back. Tamia passed the Dutch to Bourbon as she asked "Where we going cousin?"

"South Street". Tamia responded as she looked for a cd to put in.

"Take that cd out for me chick." Tamia asked.

"You always trying to Dj and drive at the same time concentrate on one thing with your multitasking self". Bourbon said as she pushed eject.

Tamia got upset when she heard laughter coming from the backseat.

"Go ahead cousin, and while you two find something funny one of y'all need to be rolling up, here go the weed and here go the Dutch, I don't care who roll."

"Too many times I been around that track and it's not just going to happen like that cause I ain't no holla back girl I ain't no holla back girl, ooh ooh that's my shit that's my shit, ooh ooh that's my shit that's my shit" as Gwen Stephani came through the speakers.

"That is my shit, cousin turn that up." Tamia said to Bourbon as she took the Dutch from Redds.

"I was already on it you see me in mid reach." Bourbon responded.

They all sang as Tamia continued up Interstate I-95 on her way to their destination.

"So what are you going to South Street for cousin?" Bourbon asked Tamia as she passed the Dutch to 2cent.

"I need to grab some shoes from dudes and an outfit from Platinum for this party tonight plus I need to pick up some change from around the corner from there." Tamia said as she grabbed the Dutch from Redds's hand.

"Who the hell rolled this shit up?" Tamia said with a look of disgust on her face after she took one pull.

"Redds." 2cent interrupted.

"Nobody ask you for your 2cent, that's why we call you 2cent now because you always putting your 2cent in something damn can I get a chance to say I rolled it." Redds barked at 2cent.

"Don't get mad at me because your ass can't roll." 2cent laughed as she sparked the Dutch she rolled.

"I know right." Bourbon added.

"What are you laughing at Tamia your rolls be fucked up too sometimes it ain't just me." Redds snapped at Tamia.

"So what I be high when I fuck it up you were sober and fucked it up so go ahead with that bullshit for real Redds." Tamia said as she passed the messed up Dutch to Bourbon.

"Just shut up and smoke" Redds barked.

"Now you mad at me because you can't roll." Tamia added.

Redds rolled her eyes even more mad she didn't have a good come back.

"Put that Hov in I need to hear that Black Album you told me to stop trying to Dj and drive but your fake ass Dj ass got me listening to the radio you know I don't listen to the radio put a cd in matter fact put that Hov in." Tamia snapped on Bourbon as she got off at the Columbus Boulevard exit.

"Go ahead cousin because we were listening to Holla Back Girl." Bourbon snapped back.

"Yeah but they went to commercial though next excuse." Tamia responded.

"I'm putting the Hov in Tamia leave me alone man." Bourbon said.

"Alright I quit." Tamia said as she made a left on to Delaware Ave.

"I keep meaning to go on the Spirit of Philadelphia I'll get there though." Tamia spoke her thoughts aloud.

"Have you ever been to Moshulu?" Bourbon asked.

"Nah but I need to get there too, that hotel is so nice I would love to own one of those." Tamia responded distracted by one of the many Landmarkson Delaware Avenue.

"I hate these brick streets." Tamia said.

"So do I cousin." Bourbon quickly agreed.

"So who party is it tonight?" Redds asked.

"My friend in Camden I'm riding over for a minute I ain't staying long though I really don't do the club scene any more that shit is getting old you feel me? Tamia answered.

"Yeah tell me about it" Redds said as they parked on South Street in front of dudes.

"What kind of shoes are you getting?" asked 2cent.

"Some hot ass Mauri's I seen the other day they mean." Tamia responded.

"I think I know what you're talking about." Bourbon said as they walked inside.

"This is what I came to get right here let me get a size nine and a half, in these." Tamia said to the manager.

"You're going to pay that much for them?" 2cent said shaking her head.

"I just like nice shit that's all we out I need to stop at Platinum now." Tamia responded.

"Look at this nigga he got his whole earlobe pierced I know that must have hurt." 2Cent said with a look of disgust on her face as they exited the store.

"I know right." Responded Redds.

"It's packed up here hey cutie you look good boy you look good." 2Cent said as a group of guys walked by.

"We can't take 2Cent nowhere cause she's a flirt don't leave your man around her cause she's a flirt." Tamia sang as everyone laughed while they walked down the next block to platinum.

"Tamia you crazy girl" Redds said.

"No 2Cent is crazy that's my girl though, look at that sexy ass nigga right there." Tamia said almost walking into the person coming towards her as she turned to look at the guy that caught her attention.

"Look at you Tamia" said 2Cent.

"Yeah but I ain't say anything to dude you did that's the difference." Tamia responded.

As they walked into Platinum 4 guys were coming out.

"Hello ladies." the finest one spoke to the girls.

"Hello sexy." Tamia said as the other girls said hi.

"What's your name mami?" The gentleman asked Tamia in a seductive tone.

"You can call me Spazz for now." Tamia whispered in his ear.

"For now? Why for now?" The gentleman asked with a confused look on his face.

"Because if I let you into my world I'll let you call me by my government." Tamia responded in a seductive tone.

Intrigued he smiled and asked for Tamia's phone number. She took his cell phone out of his hand and stored her number in it.

"What's your name?" Tamia asked.

"Ice." The gentleman responded.

"Oh Ice is it?" Tamia responded.

"Yeah if I let you into my world I'll let you call me by my government name." Ice said with a smirk on his face.

"Oh yeah? Why are you using my material on me?" Tamia asked shocked he fed off of her flirting.

"Because I like it I'll call you in a few days Spazz, you take care of yourself until I get a chance to take care of you." Ice whispered in Tamia's ear.

"I like the sound of that I'll do just that." Tamia responded.

Tamia continued in the store as they parted ways. The girls were smiling intrigued by the conversation between Ice and Tamia.

"Looks like you bagged another cutie cousin, and he's smooth, shopping in here you know he got cash." Bourbon said to Tamia.

"We'll see." Tamia responded. "That outfit you're putting together is hot." Redds said to Tamia.

"Thanks that's my skills at work, that's my skills you know I take it to Stunt Mountain at the drop of a dime baby." Tamia replied imitating Marley Marl.

"Tamia you dumb." Redds responded as they all laughed.

"That's okay I'm a fashion genius though, another fashion statement, you'll love me in the morning." Tamia said in an Al Pachino impression. The girls couldn't stop laughing.

"Come on y'all we out, I got to go pick up this change from around the corner." Tamia said as she headed out the door.

They laughed and joked all the way back to the truck. When they turned the corner they heard gun shots close by.

"I Hope that didn't come from where we're about to go." said 2Cent.

"Yeah I really don't feel like any drama today I just want to collect my money and keep it moving." Tamia responded as she sped off in the direction of her destination.

As they got closer she got a strange feeling in her stomach that something wasn't right. As Soon as she turned the corner Cash was laying on the pavement in a pool of blood.

"Damn who the fuck killed my lieutenant." Tamia thought to herself.

"Let me park around the corner so the girls won't get scared." Tamia continued to think to herself as she parked two blocks away and around the corner.

"Y'all sit tight I'll be right back I have to go holla at my man real quick." Tamia said before she exited the truck.

Relieved Bourbon asked "So that wasn't your mans we just rode pass back there or around the corner or whatever you just made a couple turns I don't know but that wasn't him?" Bourbon asked.

"No." Tamia responded.

"That's good I thought I had to be the getaway driver or something." Bourbon said as the other two girls laughed.

Tamia just shook her head and said "You crazy cousin I'll be back."

Tamia shut the door and made her way around the corner. Tamia cocked her nine millimeter and kept it concealed. Night was just beginning to fall.

"Who would make a hit in semi broad day light?" Tamia thought to herself when Flex came from out of nowhere.

"Spazz what up I'm so glad you just walked up I think that was supposed to be a hit on you they asked for Spazz, when we said Spazz ain't here what you want, where you from who sent you they thought we were lying and opened fire on Cash because they thought he was you, they didn't know you are a female they might have peeped how we operate and everyone reporting to Cash and gave their change to Cash so they thought you were him." Flex said only taking 3 breathes.

"So did any of you niggas hit any of them?" Spazz asked in an angry tone.

"What did you tell us? Tuck the hammers never keep them on us just in case fifty shows up by the time we got to our hammers a Black Suburban pulled up and they hopped in the truck I got a tag number for you though." Flex responded hoping Tamia would be pleased with that.

"Good did any of you check Cash to see if my change is still on him? Did y'all call an ambulance?" Tamia asked.

"Already on top of it boss it's all there five thousand dollars and you know how nine one one is in this city like Flavor Flav said it's a joke I called about 20 minutes ago no sirens from fifty or an ambulance." Flex responded.

"All right clean everything up before they show up hammers, work, everything and tell the rest of the workers shop closed at least for a week or two until this shit blows over make sure Cash don't have nothing on him that'll make this spot look suspicious to fifty we ain't on their radar and I want to keep it like that make them think it was a robbery or something I don't want no heat you understand me?" Spazz said in a stern voice.

"I got you Spazz." Flex responded.

"We going to get to the bottom of this shit that's one of ours they lit up but it was meant for me so that's two strikes they got against them my guess is it's some hating ass nigga that's mad our team still getting money in this drought and they can't get no work but take care of that then hit my phone when you're done the sirens should be sounding in about 15 more minutes so hurry up." Tamia said as she headed back to the truck.

"Alright boss." Flex responded before heading back towards Cash's body.

Tamia put the safety back on her nine millimeter and put it away.

"Who could be looking for me this shit is crazy but I have to find them before they find me can't let them sing me a lullaby." Tamia thought to herself.

When she finally came around the corner the girls had already rolled up and started smoking without her.

"Like that shit ain't my weed they're smoking I need new friends." Tamia thought to herself as she shook her head before she opened the door.

The truck was so full of smoke the windows were foggy.

"Damn y'all couldn't wait until I got back what the fuck you know how I feel about that shit."

Tamia snapped as she closed the door to the truck.

"Damn Tamia you did leave us in here for like twenty minutes." 2 Cent barked back.

"Twenty whole minutes you need to stop." Tamia said as she heard the sirens getting closer.

"Pass me a Dutch I know y'all been in rotation for a minute without me already so let me hit one of them." Tamia said as she pulled off and headed to the highway. Redds passed her the Dutch.

"If they knew what I know they would've passed me one as soon as I got back in the truck to calm me down after what I just seen and heard tonight, shit." Tamia thought to herself.

"Cousin, pass me that life after death cd." Tamia asked.

"Ok." Bourbon responded. Tamia took a few more pulls while Bourbon looked for the cd.

"I should take this to the head I need it." Tamia thought to herself.

"Here you go cousin." Bourbon said finally finding the cd.

Tamia passed her the Dutch as she took the cd from her. As Tamia switched cds she tried to think of which disc had the song she was looking for on it so she tried disc one.

"Why are you skipping pass all my shit." Redds snapped.

"Right." Bourbon added.

"I'll go back I need to hear something right now.

"Somebody's got to die if I go you got to go, Somebody's got to die, let the gunshots blow, Somebody's got to die nobody's got to know that I killed your ass in the midst bitch." Biggie came through the speakers as Tamia zoned out and drove.

Redds passed Tamia the Dutch as she got onto the ramp leading to the highway.

"You alright cousin is everything all right because your whole mood changed after you left and came back you straight?" Bourbon asked

"Yeah I'm good I just have some things to sort out in my head that's all I'm just thinking, Look are y'all going to this party with me tonight Or what?" Tamia asked changing the subject.

"Yeah, we going I have to find a baby sitter." 2Cent responded.

"All right, I'll drop y'all off then I know it'll be about twelve o'clock by the time y'all bitches finish getting dressed." Tamia said.

"Go ahead cousin." Bourbon snapped back offended by what Tamia said.

"Well it's the truth shit." Tamia responded.

"But it's only seven thirty." Bourbon tried to plead her case because she takes the longest to get dressed out of the three girls.

"So what my point exactly I have to tell y'all at three o'clock to be ready by nine o'clock." Tamia said.

Bourbon laughed and turned up the music while shaking her head from side to side. Tamia immediately went back into her zone as she played the song over again missing it the first time because she was talking to Bourbon.

"Somebody's got to die, if I go you got to go, somebody's got to die, Let the gunshots blow, Somebody's got to die no body's go to know that I killed your ass in the midst bitch." Biggie continued to sing as Tamia got off the Widener exit going into Chester.

On her way to Bourbon's house she snapped out of her zone. "Look its seven- fifty, are y'all going to be ready by ten o'clock?" Tamia asked.

"Yes." The girls said in unison.

"All right I'm out." Tamia said her goodbyes before she pulled off.

Meanwhile, things were still the same around the Twenty Fourth Street area. The local guys were on Dana's front steps. That was the local hang out for them while they were waiting for the fiends to come around to buy drugs from them.

"What's up old heads?" Fareed said to Saint, Green, Low key and Catch up as he approached the steps.

No one knew the reason why they called him Saint because the boy was just the opposite of that. Green got his name from always thinking about money. Low key got his name from always being low key. Catch up got his name from always running late on everything, he needed to catch up.

Fareed was your typical young boy that looked up to the local drug dealers wanting to be like them.

What's up Reedie? Saint spoke as he shook Fareed's hand.

"So when you going to give me a pack or something so I can get it like y'all getting it." Fareed responded.

"You got to wait your turn." Green interrupted.

Green didn't like Fareed at all it was just something about him that gave him a bad vibe.

"Let the young bull live I like him." Saint said coming to Fareed's defense.

Saint always had a knack for liking and putting on a lame.

"See me at the end of the week." Saint said.

"All right old head." Fareed said before he stepped off smiling from ear to ear.

As soon as he turned the corner Green started snapping at Saint.

"Why the fuck you putting that little nigga on you minus well give me that dope he going to fuck it up." Green said angrily.

"I don't really like that motherfucker but if he can bring me some paper I'm all for it." Saint responded.

As soon as the words left his mouth Tamia rode through Maddy block pass the local guys on Dana's steps. She waved at the boys as she always did. Once she was out of sight they changed the subject to her.

"Damn Tamia look good as shit I would love to hit that." Saint said.

"Me too but you know that's Mike's sister." Low Key quickly reminded him.

"Man so what I still need to hit that." Saint responded.

The argument went on until another female rode by them. Typical block talk guys are always chasing a skirt.

Meanwhile, as soon as Tamia got back to her apartment she immediately flopped on the couch. Finally getting a moment alone she had time to think about the chaos that went on in Philadelphia earlier that day.

She wondered who could be trying to kill her. She thought about Cash which was her right hand man for years. They met one day on South Street when Tamia was shopping. Cash stopped her from getting a ticket the meter maid was a couple cars down from where Tamia was parked she was doing one of her V.I.P park jobs. Thinking "I'm only running in and out I don't need to go get change then come back."

Cash rushed inside the store to get Tamia to tell her. She thought that was a good thing he had done. He could have let her get a ticket. They were tight every since then. Cash has been loyal as they come to Tamia. If Tamia isn't careful she could be next.

After she gathered her thoughts she started to get dressed for the party she was attending in a few hours. Tamia's cell phone rang.

"Everyday I'm hustling, everyday I'm hustling." Rick Ross came through the speakers of her phone.

"Hello." Tamia answered.

"What up Spazz? , How are you holding up Flex told me about Cash he gave me the license plate number of that Suburban too I had my peeps run the tag I got an address what do you want me to do?" Fats asked on the other end of the phone.

"I'm ok for now it really didn't sink in yet but what I want you to do is go check on that address for me take Flex, Hammer, and Kurt with you see if you see any of them niggas slipping like still pushing that Suburban , anything, see if Flex can identify any of them dudes." Tamia said trying not to be loud enough for the neighbors to hear her.

"All right Spazz." Fats said before hanging up the phone.

Tamia finished getting dressed then headed out the door. When Tamia drove back through Maddie block the local guys had already left. Most likely they were on their way to Crozer's Pub. Either way Tamia didn't like to deal with the local around the way guys, especially since Michelle slept with just about all of them. Michelle had a baby by almost all of the guys she slept with around there including a Sun Village guy.

The Sun Village guy left her because she was a whore but ended up cuffing that stinking bitch. Michelle was always jealous of Tamia but Tamia could care less about how Michelle felt about her because as far as she was concerned she didn't like Michelle to begin with.

It was ten minutes to ten o'clock when Tamia finally pulled up to

Bourbon's house. Tamia spoke to Bourbon's parents before going upstairs to Bourbon's room.

"Are you ready chick?" Tamia asked.

"Yup almost." Bourbon responded.

"Where are those other chicks at are they on their way?" Tamia asked already growing impatient.

"Yeah they said they were on their way they should be here in like ten to fifteen minutes." Bourbon responded.

In exactly fifteen minutes Redds and 2Cent showed up.

The girls went to the CITGO on Ninth Street to get some more Dutch Masters before they got on to I95 heading North.

The CITGO was packed when they got there, it seemed like the whole city of Chester was about to satisfy their addiction to Marijuana at the same time.

To Tamia's surprise the Twenty Fourth Street boys were at the CITGO getting there Dutch Masters also. Saint couldn't resist going over to Tamia's truck to flirt.

"Hey miss lady." Saint said with a seductive look on his face.

"Hello Saint." Tamia responded with a dry hello.

"Damn Shorty why you got to be so mean all the time? What, your man not taking care of you." Saint responded ignoring Tamia's get out of my face hint she was throwing him.

"Because I know I'm like the tenth female you tried to talk to today, I don't want to deal with a whore." Tamia responded cutting right to the chase.

"Why do I have to be all that Shorty? You should give a brother a chance, and stop giving me a bad rep you got me figured out all wrong Shorty." Saint responded refusing to give up as Bourbon got back into the truck.

"I told you I don't want a whore you should listen to a person sometimes instead of over powering the conversation all the time if you'll excuse me I have a party to attend." Tamia responded a little agitated.

"Does Mike know you smoke Shorty? I know he wouldn't approve of his little sister smoking weed." Saint said trying to get under Tamia's skin.

"Yeah he knows and besides I'm grown does your mom know you smoke?" Tamia snapped back.

"All right shorty I'm not going to hold you up any longer go ahead out and enjoy your self." Saint responded.

"Thank you." Tamia responded in a sarcastic tone.

"How many did you get?" Tamia asked Bourbon.

"I brought eight where the weed at." Bourbon responded.

"Right here, give me one." Tamia answered.

They all rolled one but only sent two in rotation before Tamia pulled off.

"So who are you going all the way to Camden to go see?" Bourbon asked.

"You'll see when we get there I have a lot on my mind I just need to smoke right now." Tamia responded as she got on to the highway.

By the time they got to the Walt Whitman Bridge both Dutch Masters were gone. They lit the other two for the rest of the ride. When they pulled up to the club the only thing they saw were Mercedes Benzes, BMW X5s, BMW 745s, stretched Hummers you name it.

Anytime Hector had a party you can expect the ballers to come out. Hectors was one of Tamia's connects little did the girls know. Once they were inside pass the metal detectors they ran into Carlos, Tony, and Ramone on their way to the V.I.P.

"Hello boys, Why are y'all blocking the door way? Excuse us." Tamia said as she brushed pass the three gentlemen.

"Hello Mami, How are you?" The guys said in unison.

"Maintaining that's all one really can do am I correct?" Tamia replied.

"That's half correct mami depending on the person one might be very good at maintaining themselves and others as well." Carlos responded looking at Tamia like he wanted to tear her clothes off.

"That is correct, now if you'll excuse me I'm going over to say hello to Hector you boys finish enjoying the party." Tamia responded.

Bourbon and 2Cent sized all of them up as the girls followed Tamia pass the gentlemen.

"You can go back and mingle with them if you want to." Tamia suggested.

"I thought you'd never ask" 2Cent said as she started walking back towards the guys.

"Yeah I thought you'd never ask." Redds agreed as she followed 2Cent over to the guys.

"I want to meet your friend first I want to see who got you coming over the bridge to come see them." Bourbon said as they walked towards Hector.

Once they made it over to the leather couch Hector was sitting on he stood up to greet the ladies.

"Hello mami glad to see you made it." Hector spoke to Tamia.

"Hello Hector how are you?" Tamia responded.

"I'm fine, who's your friend?" Hector inquired about the new face standing before him.

"Oh I'm sorry where are my manners Hector this is Bourbon, and Bourbon this is Hector." Tamia replied.

"It's nice to meet you." Hector and Bourbon both said in unison.

"Bourbon I think Carlos is trying to get your attention." Hector said.

Bourbon smiled as she turned to walk towards where Carlos was standing with Tony, 2Cent, Ramone, and Redds.

"You left me here all alone we're starting off wrong already." Carlos said as Bourbon approached him he already knew what Hector and Tamia needed to discuss so he stepped in to keep Bourbon occupied so they could talk.

Now that they were alone Tamia was happy her and Hector could talk in private.

"So what happened out there in Philly earlier today Carlos said his lieutenant and your lieutenant were good friends so tell me is this going to be bad for business or is everything under control." Hector asked.

"No it's not going to bad for business I just closed shop for a few days until this blows over some dumb young buck don't know who he's fucking with that's all, disrespecting, so I got to spank him it's nothing I still need three bricks on Thursday." Tamia responded trying not to look worried answering Hector with a poker face.

"Good I see your still on top of things waiting for things to blow over is a good idea Thursday is good I'll get word to you on Tuesday to let you know where to meet me." Hector responded.

Tamia was relieved she kept her poker face and her connect at the same time.

"Whose ever responsible for this is definitely going to get their heads blown off before this shit blows out of proportion how did it get to Hector this fast wow it only happened a few hours ago." Tamia thought to herself.

"Hey Hec what's up with the Moet why isn't it flowing we are in route to the top aren't we?" Tamia asked.

"Yes, we are." Hector replied.

"Well all right then let's have a toast to success shall we." Tamia said trying to take her mind off of the drama from earlier she signaled for the waitress to come over and when she finally made it over to where she and Hector were sitting she put in an order for five bottles.

After about ten minutes later the bottles arrived Hector popped the first one poured two glasses and made the toast shortly after both of their entourages came over to join them.

"So did you guys have enough time to mingle?" Hector asked not wanting to lead on that the conversation was serious.

"Yes we did." 2Cent responded. Hector poured more glasses then they gave a toast to life and slowly finished off all five bottles when they were done the girls were smashed. They had four Dutch Masters and five bottles of champagne. They excused themselves from the table then headed outside to the truck. Once they were inside the truck the girls were excited.

"When are we coming back over here?" 2Cent asked smiling from ear to ear.

"I don't know I'll let y'all know." Tamia responded not really wanting to bring them back over there mixing business with pleasure was always bad for business.

The girls fell asleep on the ride back to Chester. After Tamia dropped them off she headed to her apartment. Once she made it inside she collapsed on the couch the thought of the events that took place that day, replayed in her head finally having a chance to think about Cash's death she started to cry. She could only mourn alone to anyone else crying would show a sign of weakness. She cried until she finally fell asleep.

The next morning she called a meeting. Tamia phoned Fats to tell him to call the rest of the South Philly Soldiers.

"We have to have a sit down ASAP tell everyone to meet at the Charriot on Broad Street at noon." Tamia said to Fats.

"Okay boss." Fats responded before hanging up.

Tamia had a conference room paid up for a year. After Tamia hung up she started to get dressed. She didn't want to express how she was feeling through her attire so she carefully picked out her outfit. She chose a black pair of James jeans, a white button up blouse, and a Tan suede Blazer, and to top it all off a tan suede pair of stilettos to match her Blazer. Her tan suede D&G handbag made her outfit complete.

After she showered and dressed she headed out the door. When she got to the corner where Harry's and EG's were she decided to stop pass the store when she pulled in the parking lot of EG's she ran into Saint.

"Hello Miss Lady Can I get the door for you" Saint spoke. Always impressed by his manners she allowed him to open the door to her truck and the door of the store for her.

As usual he was kicking game the whole time he was walking with her.

"So when are you going to let me be your Knight in shining armor, your beast to your beauty?" Saint asked.

Not wanting to give in Tamia started singing. "I guess I'll see you next lifetime." The Erika Badu song broke the hypnotizing attraction between the two. They both enjoyed a laugh from Tamia's response.

"So it's like that huh Shorty?" Saint responded with his face red from blushing.

"Yeah it's like that." Tamia responded as she paid the store clerk. She walked away then turned to wave goodbye to Saint.

"See you Miss Lady." Saint said with a seductive look in his eyes.

That name always made Tamia melt so she quickly exited the store to get into her truck.

"I'm in a hurry anyway I have a meeting to attend no time to flirt with any around the way guys right now." Tamia thought to herself.

As she headed towards the highway she couldn't help but to notice how fast spring was approaching. Once on the highway she started to gather her thoughts together.

"I can't show any signs of weakness to my squad soldiers are only as strong as their leader." Tamia thought to herself.

She never liked Center City because of how expensive parking is in that area. But once she approached the Charriot doors she was fine.

"Good morning Miss Tamia how are you today?" One of the doormen greeted her.

"Good morning Jesus how are you as she slid him a twenty dollar bill.

"I'm good your conference room is ready for you, Miss Tamia there are pictures of water and orange juice, coffee and Danish also for you and your entourage to enjoy." Jesus responded.

"Thank you Jesus you always know how to treat a lady." Tamia responded before heading to the conference room.

Tamia always liked to be the first one there so that the soldiers would know exactly how important being punctual really is. She had a whole forty five minutes before the Soldiers were supposed to arrive. She had enough time to gather her thoughts and to think of what topics she needed to discuss. Twenty five minutes later Fats and Flex showed up looking Dapper as ever. They were trying to impress their boss by showing up early. The both of them wanted so bad to be moved up to lieutenant. They thought since Cash was dead that spot needed to be filled and they both wanted it since it was up for grabs. Trying to think ahead of their boss they figured she would want to increase the staff with more security. They were uncertain but still tried to figure out what the meeting was about before it began.

"Fats, Flex your early I didn't expect to see you for another twenty minutes." Tamia said in a surprised tone.

"We know how important this meeting is so we decided to come a little early." Flex responded happy Tamia noticed their punctuality. "Since you two are here you can fill me in on a few things like who you got sitting on that address as we speak." Tamia asked demanding an answer.

"Oh it's taken care of Hammer and Kurt both are there so you know neither one of them will be at this meeting we'll fill them in on what was discussed later." Fats responded.

"I didn't call you when I finished cleaning up the block because I hit Fats up to give him the address so he could handle that I thought that five grand was it but it wasn't here is the other ten stacks he put in his whip along with the rest of the coke it's five stacks worth of twenties and three stacks worth of dimes I put all the guns in the stash house on Bainbridge and I thought you would want the change and the work so here it all is in this bag after I finished counting it all up Fats called me to sit on that address with the rest of the soldiers and yeah I recognized the driver that nigga is related to the lookout you had Cash fire for smoking weed on the job that little nigga ain't know who was who out there Guns was posting that little nigga in the spots he was supposed to be in looking for Jake he was never in the same spot he thought Cash was you and you were his girlfriend that's how we play it with the rookies we don't tell them anything until they move up a couple of ranks so this little nigga must of ran his mouth to his people and they squadded up and came at Cash." Flex finally finished and waited for a response.

After a long pause Tamia spoke.

"So let me get this straight Guns hired this little nigga and Cash never spoke to him until he fired him?" Tamia asked.

"Yeah exactly." Flex answered scared to respond.

"I want y'all to keep sitting on the driver to see if he leads y'all to the rest of his so called squad I want this to end quickly I want the lookout and his peoples the driver whoever he is and his squad everybody lays down you hear me." Tamia said in an angry tone.

"Yes boss" Fats and Flex said in unison." As they finished the conversation the rest of the Soldiers started walking in.

"Everybody take a seat and be quiet we getting straight to the point." Tamia spoke in a stern voice. As the last soldier entered Tamia closed the ballroom door.

"Everyone knows what happened to Cash correct?" Tamia asked.

Everyone nodded in unison to agree with Tamia.

"So you know there's no lieutenant at this point right?" Tamia asked.

Everyone nodded in unison again.

"So everyone is aware that shop is closed until this all blows over right." Tamia asked.

Everyone just looked at each other. "There's going to be some changes the block Cash died on is no longer in operation the police will keep coming to the scene looking for more and more evidence we don't need that heat so when shop open back up the rest of the blocks will be open and another that I'm plotting on to replace that block if after a month goes by the cops stop their search or chase the same Suburban that we're already sitting on, then we can open that block back up until then I'm shutting it down as for the rest of you I'm disappointed in you for not handling the situation a lot better than you did, when that nigga first asked for me one or all of you within ear shot distance should've been on it, every pistol out there should've been drawn from now on that's how you handle the situation where ever you posted up at, your hammer need to be close by within three feet no one is supposed to be able to get at my team like this from now on Fats and Flex are the lieutenants for every piece of real estate that belongs to the South Philly Soldiers. I'm giving Cash's family twenty grand to bury him the rest of you need to give up some money to his family so they can be straight for a while. Every runner, every look out needs to be tested and evaluated before they get hired or promoted, As for the rest of you watch everyone under you

I can't afford any more fuck ups, my connect heard about this shit last night this shouldn't have got back to him. Guns you need to get up with Hammer and Kurt and sit on his relative of your look out you do the look out and his peoples yourself if I hear Hammer or Kurt pulled the trigger for you your finished as an SPS do you understand this meeting is adjourned." Tamia said not waiting for Guns to respond.

"Fats, Flex" Tamia called out to the two guys "Hang back for a few minutes." Tamia continued.

She waited for everyone to leave then closed the Ballroom door.

"Go see Hammer and Kurt before Guns does tell them what I said Guns is to do also tell them if he doesn't pull the trigger on them both not one but both of them sing that nigga a lullaby because he is suspect to me right now." Tamia demanded.

They looked at each other then responded. "Yes boss we're on it ASAP." They said in unison.

"Tell them in person stay off the Nextel's." Tamia said before they exited the Ballroom.

Once Tamia left the Charriot, she went straight to the stash house to take the bag Flex gave her to the house before she got on the highway to go back to the city of Chester.

CHAPTER TWO:

ANOTHER DAY, ANOTHER DOLLAR

Tamia was taller than your average female. She was five foot nine inches tall. Half black, half Indian with a caramel complexion beautiful long jet black hair down the middle of her back and thick in all the right places.

Even with sleep in her eyes she was still sexy as ever. It was eight o'clock in the morning when she was awakened by an alert from her Nextel cellular phone. First she let out a yawn then got out of bed to get her phone before answering.

"Yizzo" Tamia spoke into the speaker of her phone.

"Yo Spazz I need ten of them things when can I meet up with you I need them ASAP." An anxious Hutch came through the speaker of her phone.

"All right Hutch, meet me at the spot at like two o'clock nigga I'm trying to get some shut eye." Tamia said half sleep.

"Ok Spazz, what you had a rough night last night or something, a tool and a hangover will do that to you." Hutch said joking with Tamia.

"Shut up nigga I'll see you at two o'clock." Tamia said before she put the phone down.

Tamia wasted no time going back to sleep. After all she did take a trip to New York the day before to get five trash bags of marijuana.

Tamia supplied the whole city of Wilmington in the State of Delaware. Some parts of Chester, PA and of course some parts of New Jersey. No one in her hometown of Chester knew exactly how large she really was except for Sanaa and that's exactly how Tamia wanted to keep it.

Sanaa was also taller than your average female. She stood five foot ten inches tall with a slim frame. She had a caramel complexion with Chinese eyes and shoulder length jet black hair. She was definitely a sight for soar eyes. Tamia and Sanaa had been best friends since the age of twelve. Eighteen years later they were still closer than ever. Sanaa and Tamia were both hairstylist. They opened a beauty shop together as soon as they graduated from Gordon Phillips Beauty School. Tamia only took appointments while Sanaa took walk in clients and appointments.

They had two other stylist working in their shop Shantel and Shawna. They took mainly walk in clients because they were still trying to build their clientele up since the day they started a year ago.

Tamia and Sanaa had Chester on lock with their shop. You name it they sold it. From packs of weave, Spritz, Oil sheen to Perfume, Cologne, Handbags, Scarves, and Do rags, whatever your preference was, they had it for sale.

While Tamia was in New York she not only got a connection for some good marijuana. She came across some wholesalers for the products they sold in the shop also. When they first opened the shop up, into their first two years they struggled hard to keep the shop open refusing to let the people who thought negatively about them opening a shop together so soon after they graduated, be right about everything they were saying, so Tamia stepped up and got into the drug game. A game that we really shouldn't be calling a game because it's not fun when you get booked and your new address is a cell in the County, State, or federal jail. It's not fun if your game over is death. Nor is it fun when you have to take a life. In the streets only the strong survive and Tamia was the stronger of the two friends.

As far as anyone in Chester knew Tamia made most of her money at the shop. Tamia and Sanaa made sure Spoiled Br@ Hair Technicians was the Talk of the Tri-State. They came up with the name because they both were spoiled rotten. Tamia kept Bourbon, Redds, and 2Cent away from Sanaa and her away from them because Sanaa didn't like them, and they didn't like her. The three girls went to the shop to get their hair done every now and again but not too often. All five girls hanging out, was definitely out of the question. After the wholesaler Spoiled Br@ Hair Technicians was the top Beauty Salon in the Tri-State area.

When ten o'clock rolled around Tamia finally got up to get dressed. After all she did have inventory to do at the shop and bag up the five trash bags of marijuana she got the day before so she can make her two o'clock appointment with Hutch.

"Damn, another day, another dollar but fuck it I need to get this paper." Tamia thought to herself as she yawned making her way to the shower.

After she got out of the shower she picked an outfit to wear then started to lotion herself down. Just as she finished putting lotion down those long thick legs of hers.

"Bitch wake up, what you forgot you were supposed to be meeting me at the shop at eleven o'clock." Sanaa came through the direct connect of Tamia's Nextel.

"My bad S I'm on my way right now I'm getting dressed." Tamia answered back.

"Hurry up bitch you always talking about somebody being punctual you ain't being punctual right now it's eleven o'clock I'm here you ain't here." Sanaa said knowing she was getting on Tamia's nerves.

"Shut the fuck up bitch I had a long day yesterday remember, that long ass ride to New York you didn't want to take with me? So fall back with all that and sit tight I'll be there in fifteen minutes, all right." Tamia responded as she finished getting dressed.

As she headed to the shop things were unusually deserted on Maddy block and Twenty Fourth Street, she figured the police must have been patrolling early in the area.

When she pulled up in front of the shop she saw Sanaa through the window already stocking the shelves with the hair products Tamia brought back the day before.

"So are you going to help me or what?" Sanaa asked as soon as Tamia walked in the door.

"Yeah, after I weigh up a few pounds of this weed I have a sell to make at two o'clock plus bitch you did skip out on the trip you can stock that shit yourself." Tamia responded.

"I was only joking but we are supposed to be going over the books together and do inventory so go handle your business Mia." Sanaa said feeling a little guilty for being selfish.

Tamia then went into the office and shut the door. After about Forty five minutes she came back out.

"Okay look either we can go over the books now or you can wait until I come back." Tamia said.

"I'll wait I don't want you to rush through it trying to get to your sell." Sanaa responded.

Tamia helped Sanaa stock the shelves until it was time for her to leave.

"Okay I'm out I'll be back in a little bit." Tamia said as she walked out the door.

Tamia got in her Escalade and took the long way to Wilmington. Once she drove through Marcus Hook she decided to stop pass the liquor store on Naamans Road. She knew when she got back Sanaa was going to be expecting some type of alcoholic beverage. She got a bottle of Patron, a half gallon of orange juice and a few bottles of Moet then headed down Philadelphia Pike to Wilmington. When she pulled up to the pool Hutch was already there waiting.

"Hutch your early Do I need to count that here?" Tamia asked always suspicious of everyone.

"You know me, has my money ever been funny with you in the last five years?" Hutch responded somewhat offended.

"No but I still like to count you never know in this game." Tamia said easing the tension that was building up inside of Hutch.

"You right Spazz besides I'm completely out of weed so I need to go bag up ASAP." Hutch responded.

"Tell Starsky to hit me up tonight if he needs to re-up today I'll be tied up for the next few hours." Tamia said.

"Okay one love Spazz." Hutch said as he exited the truck.

"One, oh and Hutch this count better be right if this ain't sixty five hundred I'll be back sooner nigga." Tamia said before she pulled off.

She headed for Interstate 495. It took her twenty minutes to get to the Kerlin street exit. She headed straight to the shop Eighth Street was packed as usual but Tamia kept going to the next block and pulled over in front of the shop. As soon as she got inside she locked the door behind her then headed straight for the back to count the money Hutch had given her in the office.

After she counted the money it was actually five hundred over. So Tamia then immediately got Hutch back on the phone.

"What's up Spazz, I know that shit ain't short ma." Hutch said.

"Nah it ain't short Hutch it's actually five hundred over you gave me seven thousand." Tamia responded.

"I know keep it that's my gift to you for keeping a nigga pockets all swollen for the last five years a hundred for each year we been doing business together." Hutch said showing his appreciation.

"So I guess this is connect appreciation week huh Hutch." Tamia responded with a chuckle.

"You know it, go buy yourself a pair those fly ass Mauri's you be wearing ma." Hutch said sounding like he was real proud of himself.

"All right hutch thanks baby boy." Tamia responded.

Hutch could tell she was blushing on the other end. After she put the money in the safe she joined Sanaa out front.

"Are you ready to go over the books now Mia?" Sanaa asked as soon as she opened the door.

"Yeah I'm ready how much did these chicks bring in this week with rent and products that they sold to their clients?" Tamia asked. It's always business first with her.

"Ok first of all you and I made twelve hundred a piece selling products to clients and the girls made six hundred between the two of them on top of their two hundred for their weekly rent. Besides what we made individually that's a total of thirty four hundred." Sanaa said hoping her partner was pleased with how business was going.

"All right that's cool but we have to increase our clientele how bout we hire a barber to bring some men in here to spend some money I mean guys with braids aren't the only ones that wear do-rags we can push some cologne to them also maybe start selling wallets, white tees, wife beaters, and socks to them too." Tamia suggested.

"Yeah I think it's a good idea but you know this is our slow week though." Sanaa responded.

"Yeah exactly my point I don't want a slow week at all." Tamia answered.

"Listen Mia I need you here this week coming because you know this is our busy week and you know Shantel and Shawna are slow so I'm going to need help with some of the walk ins I know your probably booked but your days off can you please come in?" Sanaa pleaded.

"Okay Sanaa but won't you give me a wet set real quick boo." Tamia asked.

"Sure if I can play with you while you're under the dryer." Sanaa said with a seductive smile on her face.

Tamia couldn't help but to smile they've been secretly seeing each other for the last eight years no one knew that either one of them were bi-sexual.

"You are so nasty come wash my hair girl." Tamia said shaking her head.

"So I take that as a yes." Sanaa said excitedly.

"Ooh what's in the bag is that? Yes it is thank you Mia can I take a shot of this Patron first? What's the Moet for? What are we celebrating? Sanaa said throwing a series of questions Tamia's way.

Tamia popped one of the bottles and poured two glasses.

"To us to a lifelong friendship and ten years of being Successful business partners not to mention our relationship I don't know what I would do without you Sanaa I love you." Tamia said giving the toast.

"Cheers to us." Sanaa said before she clanged glasses with Tamia then they drank.

After the second glass Tamia's phone rang.

"Hello." Tamia answered.

"Hello sexy how have you been?" A familiar voice said on the other end.

"Thanks for the compliment but who am I speaking with?" Tamia asked.

"This is Ice your future husband sexy." Ice answered.

"Oh Ice hello how are you?" Tamia answered trying to shake the buzz she had so he wouldn't hear it in her voice.

"I'd be doing just fine if I could take you out tonight or is this too short of notice?" Ice asked hoping to get a yes out of Tamia.

"So what do you have in mind?" Tamia replied.

"Well for starters we can meet at Fat Tuesday's on South St. for a few drinks and go from there." Ice responded.

"That sounds like a plan I guess I'll see you tonight what time would you like to meet up?" Tamia asked.

"About nine o'clock." Ice answered. "Should I store this number or do you have another one for me to store?" Tamia asked.

"You can store this one sexy see you then, later sexy." Ice answered before they hung up the phone.

As soon as Tamia hung up she was staring in the face of an angry Sanaa.

"What?" Tamia asked hesitantly.

"Who was that you know damn well I need to screen your dates so who is this Ice and when do I get to meet him?" Sanaa said all in one breathe.

"Soon let me screen him first can you get started on my hair so I can tell you the little bit of details there is because this is our first date." Tamia said pleading her case.

"Come on let me wash your hair." Sanaa responded then headed to the sink with Tamia following closely behind her.

"Sit down is this water too hot for you?" Sanaa asked.

"No it's fine, so when are you going to start back dating again Sanaa?"

Tamia asked realizing Sanaa hasn't been dating much in the last six months. "I will when I find someone that's worth it." Sanaa responded.

"I hear you girl." Tamia said while enjoying the head massage Sanaa was giving her while she washed her hair.

"So describe this Ice character." Sanaa asked being curious about who her girlfriend was about to go out on a date with.

"Oh S he's about six foot two inches tall wavy jet black hair a caramel complexion and the way his clothes hang off of him you can tell he's a gym rat I hope he has a brain because I can't wait to rip his clothes off." Tamia described him to Sanaa as they made their way over to the styling chair.

"So where did you two meet?" Sanaa inquired as she started to put the rollers in her hair.

"The same place as our first date is going to take place on South St. he was coming out of Platinum and I was going in with Bourbon, Redds, and 2cent." Tamia said before Sanaa interrupted.

"I don't know why you hang with them weed smoking no ambition having broke ass losers. They going to bring you down to their level Mia and I don't want that for you we been friends for too long and now that I've been tasting you for some time now I feel a lot closer to you. I only want the best for you." Sanaa said showing concern for her friend.

"Yeah but." Tamia responded trying to explain.

"But nothing cut them bitches off for real I don't like them anyway." Sanaa said cutting Tamia off once again.

"That's why I keep you away from them and them away from you. Anyway before you interrupted me, this nigga said take care of yourself until I get a chance to take care of you before he walked away from me. Girl I never heard that line before." Tamia said.

"Me either I'm done it's time for you to get under the dryer." Sanaa said.

After Sanaa set the dryer she wasted no time unbuttoning Tamia's pants after she sat under the dryer. Tamia couldn't help but to grin looking at how beautiful Sanaa was her five foot ten inch slim frame bent towards her with that silk caramel skin and her jet black hair in her face finally getting her pants off bending back Tamia's leg and helping herself to her already dripping wet vagina. Tamia enjoyed every minute of it as she looked down at Sanaa she saw her Chinese shaped eyes seductively looking back at her she became more aroused. After Sanaa stuck her fingers inside of Tamia hitting her G-spot Tamia exploded all over her fingers and the chair. When Sanaa finished making Tamia orgasm she licked her fingers then went to get a towel to wash off Tamia and the chair.

"Thank you S I needed that I been so stressed lately." Tamia said relieved she let that tension out.

"I can always tell I know everything about you even your cycle bitch you'll be on next week you got some pads already." Sanaa said as they both enjoyed a laugh.

Sanaa took a few minutes to clean up. When she came back the dryer shut off then she took the rollers out of Tamia's hair.

"Do you want it wrapped or are you going to wear it like this." Sanaa asked.

"No wrap it Boo, I have to take a shower before my date." Tamia responded.

"Okay Mia." Sanaa said as she started to wrap her hair.

After Tamia's hair was finished they drank the rest of the Moet then headed out the door.

"See you tomorrow Sanaa." Tamia said as she got in her truck.

"Okay Mia smooches." Sanaa responded before she got into her CLS 500 and drove off.

Tamia drove straight home to get ready for her date. As soon as she opened the door her Pit bull Rage started barking trying to let Tamia know he had to go to the bathroom. Tamia let him out of his cage grabbed his leash and headed out the door. It seemed like everybody's dog was on a timer but in that complex who knew. When Rage was done they headed back inside then Tamia got in the shower. She then ironed a D&G outfit that she got from Platinum. She combed down her hair and headed towards the door to go and meet her date on South Street. When she got near the exit she rang his Cell phone to see where he was.

"Hey sexy" Ice answered.

"Hello handsome do you answer the phone like that to every female that calls your phone?" Tamia asked in a flirtatious way.

"No just when you call." Ice responded. "I'm almost at Fat Tuesdays I just got off of the South Street exit coming from seventy six, Where are you?" Tamia asked

"I'm home waiting on your call." Ice responded.

"Oh I doubt that so are you on your way?" Tamia said.

"I am now sexy I'll see you in a half hour." Ice said before walking out of his Condo on Delaware Avenue.

"Ok." Tamia said before she hung up the phone.

"How can anyone be that smooth?" She thought to herself as she weaved in and out of traffic.

South Street was packed as ever when she finally made it down to the other end.

"I never seen it this packed up here on a Monday." Tamia thought to herself as she parked up the street from Fat Tuesday's surprised she found a parking spot so close.

She put the alarm on then headed towards the bar to meet her date. When she walked in she spotted Ice right away.

"Wow you look good in that outfit I never been in here I just normally walk pass." Tamia said as she greeted Ice with a hug.

"That is unbelievable that you never been in here you have to try there one ninety octane you'll love it." Ice said as he headed over to the bar to order them some drinks before Tamia tried to back out of tasting the drink.

"So what do you do for a living Ms. Spazz?" Ice asked as he handed Tamia her drink before he sat down at the table.

"I'm a hairstylist slash technician" Tamia responded as she took a sip of her drink.

"Oh, you're a hairstylist slash technician are you? That sounds serious." Ice responded.

"I know don't it?" Tamia asked. They both enjoyed a laugh.

"What about you Mr. Ice what do you do for a living?" Tamia asked after she gained her composure.

"Well I build houses and I have a used car lot in South Philly so if you ever need a car I got you covered sexy." Ice answered with a smile.

"Oh an entrepreneur huh I like that in a man." Tamia said continuing to flirt.

"Same here do you own your own shop or do you work for someone?" Ice inquired.

"My girlfriend and I own the shop." Tamia answered proudly.

"Oh, ok where is it located?" Ice asked grabbing her hand.

"Oh it's in Chester." Tamia answered looking into his eyes.

"So how long have you been building houses?" Tamia asked continuing the conversation.

"Well I've been into the construction business since the age of eighteen and after ten years. I started my own construction company I've been getting a lot of city contracts to build new developments and as far as the car lot I've been doing that for only two years now." Ice answered.

"So how old are you if you don't mind me asking." Tamia asked intrigued by what she's heard so far.

"I'm thirty five sexy and how old are you twenty three?" Ice asked trying to flatter Tamia.

"No silly but thank you for the compliment I'm thirty and I've been doing hair since I was like fourteen but my girlfriend started at twelve she taught me then when we were sixteen we decided to open a shop after graduation so we went to school to get our licenses after we graduated from Gordon Phillips we did just that. We were saving for it ever since the age of sixteen grinding it out doing hair in our mom's kitchens." Tamia explained.

"That's interesting I'm intrigued so you and your girlfriend are go getters huh I like that in a female, so what's your girlfriends' name?" Ice asked.

"Her name is Sanaa." Tamia said with a smile on her face thinking about the episode in the shop earlier that evening.

"So do you have any kids sexy?" Ice asked.

"No I do not and you." Tamia asked.

"Yes I have a four year old son." Ice responded proud to be a father.

"Does he have his fathers' pretty hair and bedroom eyes?" Tamia asked seductively.

"I'll let you be the judge of that if I decide to let you into my world." Ice said with a smirk on his face.

"Stop using my material boy." Tamia responded with laughter.

"Ok if you stop being so sexy." He replied.

"I can't help it, so what part of Philly are you from? Or, Are you originally from Philly?" Tamia asked.

"I'm originally from West Philly now I live in South Philly I have custody of my son so you don't have to worry about any baby momma drama or anything like that. My mom helps out and so does my sister when I need a baby sitter or have toddler questions. So what about you are you from Chester or do you just live there?" Ice asked.

"Born and raised so you know I have that C-Pride in me." Tamia said always representing where she's from like everyone from Chester usually does when they're away from home.

"Oh C-Pride is it I kind of like that I heard about that C-Pride that means you're a rider and I know for sure you got my back." Ice said trying to impress Tamia with what he knows about her city.

"Wow you did your homework I like that. Sorry I can't stay a little longer, but I just wanted to meet with you to get to know you a little more to see what you are about. And I see this could go somewhere so I'll be giving you a call real soon." Tamia said as she stood up to leave.

"Why are you leaving so soon? I was enjoying your company." Ice said with a disappointed look on his face as he stood up also.

"Well I have a big day tomorrow. I have ten appointments starting at eight in the morning so I have to get some shut eye." Tamia explained.

"Ok I can respect that as long as you're not blowing me off for another dude, I'm good." Ice said relieved.

"No never another dude just business, so I'll call you later." Tamia said as she started for the door.

"Sure let me show you my gentleman side and walk you to your car so where are you parked sweetheart?" Ice said as he followed Tamia to the door.

"That's my Escalade up the block before you get to Jim's Steak shop see it?" Tamia asked as she pointed in that direction.

"Oh ok your balling a little bit you don't need anything from my car lot huh." Ice said impressed with what Tamia was driving.

"You never know I might need a little hoopty." Tamia replied joking.

Tamia hit the alarm and when they got to the truck Ice opened the door for her so she can get in.

Impressed by his gesture she seductively said "Thank you I'll call you when I get a break tomorrow."

She pulled off and he walked back to his Jaguar and drove off. As soon as she turned the corner she called Sanaa immediately to tell her all the details. Sanaa was all ears for her girlfriend.

The next day it was business as usual the shop was packed early, filled with mostly appointments. All the clients that went to Tamia knew that if they wanted to catch her they needed to make an appointment on Tuesday, Wednesday, or Thursday because Friday and Saturday were her days off. Sunday and Monday she had inventory and made runs to New York for the shop. Little did they know she ran around the Tri-State supplying the community with the purest cocaine and the strongest marijuana a fiend and pothead could ever buy?

Shantel and Shawna were so jealous of Tamia and Sanaas' work schedules and clientele that you could feel the tension in the air.

"So when are you going to let me get some of that money Sanaa? ,You pushing a CLS 500 it ain't like you need it, always popping bottles and dressing all fly like you all that." Shawna started.

"You can always find another shop to do hair out of and I can always find another stylist." Sanaa snapped back. She never bit her tongue and that always ended the conversation.

"So Tamia why are you pushing an Escalade while Sanaa is pushing a CLS 500 ain't yall partners?" Shawna asked.

She always tried to find a way to start an argument between those two, when the argument between her and Sanaa never worked in her favor.

But trying to stir things up never worked either yet she still continued to try.

"Well Sanaa obviously has more clientele than I do and I am so proud at how successful my best friend has become." Tamia said as she smiled at Sanaa.

"Look at you Sanaa all grown up come over here and give mommy a hug." Tamia joked as the girls burst out into laughter.

"Well I don't see what's so funny I would be mad if my partner pushed a better whip than me shoot." An angry Shawna said as she rolled her eyes.

"What did I tell you about rolling your eyes don't make me send you outside for a switch keep it up?" Tamia said still joking with the girls.

"Tamia I don't find you funny." Shawna said as she rolled her eyes again.

"Then shut up and do hair that's what you're here for noodle not to be in our business. You need to think about how you can get your clientele up so you won't be so jealous." Tamia said being serious.

"It sounds like somebody's a little power struck just wait until I get both you bitches robbed see how much mouth you have then, so what y'all eating y'all can afford to give us some of y'all clientele but y'all got the game fucked up talking to me like that just wait all of that money going to be mine watch." Shawna thought to herself.

Shantel looked at Shawna and knew exactly what she was thinking because she was plotting the same thing since day one. Tamia's cell phone rang.

"Hello." Tamia answered

"Spazz it's me Hector can you talk right now?" Hector asked on the other end.

"Sure give me one minute, excuse me Keona I need to take this if you don't mind." Tamia said really telling her not asking her.

"Sure go right ahead." Keona responded.

She had been Tamia's client for seven years and was used to her being on the phone a lot. Tamia went in the office and shut the door.

"What's up Hec? Are we still on for tomorrow or what?" Tamia asked picking up the conversation again.

"Yeah Spazz but I need to get with you early like seven in the morning I have a lot to do tomorrow so come to the club." Hector responded.

"No problem I'll be there at seven." Tamia said before she hung up the phone. As she returned to her client all eyes were on her.

"Damn y'all some nosey bitches, what? I know y'all want to know what that was about but mind your business." Tamia said irritated by the attention she was getting.

Everyone did exactly that because they knew she never talked about her personal business in the shop if she told Sanaa she told her in private. There was regular shop talk for the rest of the day. What stars had a new look, needed to change their look, who got married, divorced, who's dating now, who broke up, and who has a hot new song out. Those were the only topics allowed to be talked about in their shop. Tamia and Sanaa didn't allow local gossip in their shop.

After the shop closed Tamia and Sanaa went to Upscale Tuesdays in Old City to have a few drinks and to discuss future plans for their business, they were about their money day in and day out.

The next morning Tamia got up and met up with Hector. She went in with a book bag full of money and came out with a book bag full of cocaine.

CHAPTER THREE:

BUSINESS AS USUAL

After a long week Tamia called Fats and Flex to get a briefing on the outcome with Guns.

"What's up Spazz? What took you so long to call I got some news for you?" Fats answered.

"All right Fats meet me at the spot and tell Flex I want to see him too." Tamia said before she hung up the phone.

After an hour Fats and Flex showed up.

"So what's the situation?" Tamia asked.

"Well the good news is Guns hit both of them niggas up and the other three. Now the bad news is Cash's mom had a nervous breakdown and the flip side to all of that bad news the blocks are missing money. Our competition is out of dope they caught a bad break and brought some garbage now their fiends are coming to us and shop closed. So when we setting shop back up my pockets hurting right now everybody's been in them this week." Fats answered.

"Enough said, we're back open right now I need fifteen back from both of you. I don't need any more fuck ups so be careful who you hire and when that change ready hit me you both should be done in like two or three days." Tamia said as she handed each of them Twenty thousand dollars worth of bagged up twenties.

Both the boys looked at each other and smiled.

"All right spazz thanks." They both said in unison.

"Things are going to be handled a little different now. I'm not picking up any more money from the blocks. I give you two the work you meet me at the spot to give me my money are we clear on that, nobody sees my face but you two." Tamia said

"Yeah Spazz we got you." They both said in unison as they walked out the door.

Fats and Flex were as happy as a fat kid in a candy store. They knew with the increase in clientele, the package Tamia had given them would be done by night fall.

Tamia got in her Escalade and headed to her new stash house to bag up the three bricks she just got the morning before. She didn't trust Fats and Flex as much as she did Cash so she moved her stash house somewhere else that only she knew about. She was still sitting on about sixty thousand dollars worth of bagged up dope so she decided to only bag up one brick. After a few hours had passed Tamia's phone rang.

"What's up S?" Tamia answered.

"Look we kind of busy I need you." Sanaa said getting straight to the point.

"Ok I'm in the middle of something I'll be there in like two hours." Tamia responded before she hung up the phone.

Tamia sped up her process so she could go and help Sanaa also make herself some new clientele. After an hour passed she headed for the door leaving the other two kilos untouched. After a long morning and afternoon Tamia finally showed up to the shop around Three o'clock and by the end of the day she and the other girls were exhausted. As soon as Shawna and Shantel left at twelve thirty in the morning Tamia got an unexpected text message which read "We're done." Tamia couldn't believe her eyes. Sanaa noticed the stunned look on her face and asked what was wrong.

"Nothing's wrong." Tamia responded as she sent back a text message that read I'll be there in forty five minutes.

The two partners then started to clean up the shop and about a half hour later Tamia headed out the door.

"Damn both of these niggas are done already I know they said the competition was out of product but damn they got the blocks popping like that." Tamia thought to herself very impressed with how fast the boys were finished.

She didn't think twice about it and got on I95 North bound to Philadelphia. Tamia's cell phone rang on the way there.

"What's up?" Tamia answered.

"Damn you could've said bye bitch." Sanaa snapped.

"I'm sorry I was in a rush I have to make a run real quick goodbye Sanaa smooches I'll see you tomorrow ok." Tamia responded sarcastically.

"Ok smart ass I'll see you tomorrow you be careful." Sanaa responded.

"I will." Tamia said before hanging up.

"Damn I knew I should've got up earlier to bag that dope up now I got to spend all day tomorrow bagging those other two bricks up damn I miss Cash he usually took care of half the bagging." Tamia thought to herself as she pulled up in front of the stash house.

She grabbed two packs worth twenty grand and thought maybe she should give them double this time to hold them over until she finished bagging those bricks up. She then grabbed two more and headed to the other house to meet Fats and Flex.

"If these niggas do eighty thousand between the two of them within the next two days I might need more bricks something told me to get six." Tamia thought to herself as she pulled in front of the other house.

"So are you shocked." Fats asked. "Of course I'm shocked y'all finished a day early." Tamia responded with a look of disbelief on her face.

They both handed her fifteen thousand dollars each.

"See we handling our business you picked the right two to move up and take Cash spot and we not going to let you down." Flex added.

"Ok we'll see I'm doubling up on y'all two packs a piece this time thirty back Tamia responded saying exactly what they wanted to hear. Which meant more money for them and what they had planned they were going to need it.

They parted ways so Tamia headed to her apartment to take a nap because she needed it she had a long day ahead of her.

Meanwhile Fats and Flex got right back to the block. They were on a mission like their lives depended on it. After a couple of Red Bulls they were wired enough to stay up a lot longer. Tamia woke up at ten o'clock in the morning and wasted no time getting dressed. She went straight to the stash house to bag the other two kilos and to tell Hector she needed to see him. She made arrangements to meet with him the next morning. After she finished bagging one kilo she got back to back text messages both saying we're done.

"Damn what the fuck are they doing giving this shit away?" Tamia thought to herself.

She ran over to the other house to make the exchange then headed back to finish the other Kilo. Tamia needed help in the worst way but the only person she trusted was Sanaa at this point. She lost a lot of sleep trying to juggle her Cocaine and Marijuana business on top of the shop. It took Tamia a little over a month to get a handle on the chaos that hit her as soon as she went back to business as usual after Cash was murdered.

As the weeks went by her orders were increasing with Hector and before she knew it she was a lot larger than she wanted to be. Tamia never wanted to be big time because she knew how much attention blowing up too fast could bring but it was too late to turn back. She needed to find a way out and fast. She knew whatever the plan was she had to slowly back away because too many people were involved that depended on her to make money so just quitting wasn't an option. In the middle of her routine bagging session 2Cent came through her direct connect.

"What you don't fuck with nobody no more you don't call nobody or nothing." 2Cent said without alerting her first.

"I been busy you know I'm a workaholic." Tamia responded.

"I was just playing what's up with you though you going to Celebrity Sunday tonight at Xandu?" 2Cent asked.

"Of course Celebrity Sunday wouldn't be right without this celebrity." Tamia said confidently.

"I knew your conceited ass was going to say that all right we going but Bourbon said we might just meet you there because you always complain when we aren't ready." 2cent responded.

"That sounds like a plan y'all do that." Tamia responded as she went back to work.

When she finally finished she went to her apartment to take a nap before she got dressed to go to Xandu. Tamia woke up from her slumber to get dressed. The first thing she did was grab one of the Louis V outfits she picked up from New York on her last trip. As she ironed her clothes she knew she was going to shut Celebrity Sunday down. With that outfit, hers was going to be the best Nightlife link photo of the night.

Since she was going to the club by herself she put the Escalade up and pulled out the CLK. The only person that ever rode in or even seen that Benz who knew her was Sanaa. The car was a powder blue color with white interior and Louis Vuitton on selected parts of the interior which set off the wood grain. Her custom Benz was the sharpest in the Tri-State area period.

Once she pulled on to Delaware Ave., she ran into traffic the whole way down the strip as she made her way to the club. As she drove pass she noticed Cavanaugh's was packed and so was Xandu which made parking scarce.

Tamia made a U-Turn and parked in the V.I.P spot out in front. Once she got out of the car and made her way to the front of the line outside of the club everyone was stunned when they saw her outfit all eyes were on her. The crowd became very angry when they saw her speak to the bouncers then walk right in without showing I.D or getting searched.

When she got inside she looked at how unusually packed the club was so soon. Xandu usually didn't get packed until around eleven thirty. It was eleven o'clock and everybody who was anybody in Chester, Philly, Delaware, and South Jersey were in the house that night. After she ordered a drink someone from Nightlife link was right behind her asking to take her picture when she turned around. After she took a photo she liked she made her rounds speaking to everyone she knew inside the club. At twelve o'clock she noticed Bourbon, 2Cent, and Reds were just walking in the door.

"I thought they weren't going to be here until at least one or quarter after I guess they fooled me." Tamia thought to herself. After speaking to a few more people her three associates found her.

"What's up cousin?" Bourbon asked.

"Ain't shit same ole same ole trying to make a million out of fifteen cent." Tamia responded.

"I hear that." Redds added to the conversation.

"What's up with y'all?" Tamia asked.

"Same shit." They said in unison.

What Tamia didn't know was Sanaa was also in the club. Sanaa never saw Tamia nor the other three girls walk in until she noticed Tamia talking to the three girls from Chester she hated with a passion. She didn't like them talking to what she liked to refer to as her pussy. All hell was about to break loose inside of Xandu.

"Oh yeah we seen this Benz outside that was powder blue with Louis Vuitton on the interior girl that thing was hot I hope I meet the nigga pushing that shit." 2Cent said after a few minutes of silence.

"Damn you looking inside of people cars you nosey." Tamia responded not letting the cat out of the bag about that being her Benz they were drooling over.

"Well when I find out who car that is I might need to holla at that nigga." Redds added. As soon as she finished her sentence Sanaa walked up and started snapping.

"Mia what the fuck you doing talking to these losers, these bitches ain't even on your level. I don't know why you keep these bitches around you anyway they ain't ever going to be shit but the fucking chicken heads that they are. I wish you cut them the fuck off." Sanaa said without taking a breath.

"Bitch we ain't no fucking losers fuck you bitch so what you do hair. If it wasn't for my cousin you wouldn't be eating like you eating she's the one that got the Connect to the supplies y'all selling in that shop, don't ever forget that." Bourbon quickly snapped back.

"I know right this bitch think she better than everybody because she driving a CLS so the fuck what you a fake ass bitch that can't nobody stand and that car ain't going to change that bitch." Redds added.

"CLS 500 get it right bitch and yes the fuck people can stand me y'all three are the only ones that can't stand me and I see why because y'all some jealous ass bitches. If I was y'all broke ass bitches I would hate me too." Sanaa returned the low blow.

"Cousin I don't know why you fuck with this stuck up bitch in the first place." Bourbon angrily directed her attention to Tamia as she grabbed Sanaa and escorted her to the V.I.P room.

"Look S I'm cool with them why you always tripping?" Tamia asked trying to Calm Sanaa down.

"You know I'm jealous of any female your close to I want to be the only one you confide in. I don't want them bitches to know what I know about you and I don't like them because they ain't about shit all they do is smoke weed all day." Sanaa answered as she rolled her eyes.

"Yeah but they have jobs too it ain't like they don't work losers don't even do that don't you think that was a little harsh." Tamia said trying to reason with her.

"So what I don't like them." Sanaa said as she pouted.

"Yeah but I'm going to need you to chill out on them ok, can you do that for me they don't know everything you know about me and they never will ok?" Tamia said reassuring her.

As much as Sanaa hated it she said ok. Tamia ordered a bottle of champagne after Sanaa was completely calm they went back out to the rest of the club.

"Now, where did these bitches go at that quick, I need to calm them down too I know they might try to jump her tonight when she leave if I'm not with her." Tamia thought to herself.

After forty five minutes passed Tamia assumed they left. Shawna and Shantel were in the club also they over heard the argument but went unseen by all the parties involved in the argument. They left right behind Bourbon, 2Cent and Redds.

Once outside Shawna and Shantel went straight to the three friends and started talking them over to their side the more people the better so they thought. They told them how they over heard their argument inside the club and that they couldn't stand Sanaa either. They told them what they were plotting already. Without hesitation the three friends let hate, jealousy, greed, and envy persuade them into joining Shawna and Shantel in their plot against Sanaa and Tamia, especially Sanaa.

"Last call, last call, order your drinks now the bar is closing in fifteen minutes. Last call came through the speakers. Tamia usually used that as her cue to leave. She didn't like the let out scene. It was the waiting in line to get out the door, the parking lot traffic and the line to get your coat from the coat check when it's cold that she couldn't stand.

"Look Sanaa I think you should leave now with me I'm going to follow you home to make sure you get there safe you're drunk so come on." Tamia said hoping Sanaa didn't give her a hard time.

"I'm cool but if you say so let's go." Sanaa answered.

"Alright come on." Tamia said as she grabbed Sanaa's hand.

"Where them losers go because I know they want to fight and I'm all for it." Sanaa said as she officially started ramming off of the alcohol.

"They left now come on." Tamia responded.

So she thought, they had a surprise waiting for Sanaa and wanted to see the look on her face when she saw it. They parked somewhere that wasn't out in the open so they can watch her reaction from a distance.

"Where are you parked S?" Tamia asked.

"I'm in the V.I.P spot out front." Sanaa responded.

"Ok your parked where I am, cool." Tamia said as she escorted Sanaa in the direction of the parking lot.

When they got twenty feet away from Sanaa's car she sobered up real quick.

"What the fuck? I'm going to kill these bitches." Sanaa screamed aloud.

All four tires were flat. Every window was busted out and there were traces of key scratches all over the car.

"Mia I swear to god, you need to choose and you need to choose right now either it's me or them, look at this petty shit they into I don't want them around you because I don't want them to bring you down, it's for your well being, and if they did this shit to me what make you think, they won't get mad and do this shit to you, fuck this shit if you don't stop fucking with them bitches right now, this is the end of our friend-ship, our relationship, and our business we can sell the shop and go our separate ways, so what's it going to be." Sanaa said as she folded her arms waiting for an answer.

Tamia stood silent as she stared at Sanaa's car. She noticed a brick with a note attached to it in the front seat. She went to get it to see what it said.

The note read:

"Do you see how quickly your CLS became CL SHIT? Looks like you're the LOSER now, because you just lost your precious Benz, BITCH."

After Tamia read the note aloud she looked at Sanaa still standing there with her arms folded still waiting for an answer.

"Look S you know damn well I'm not going to throw everything away that we both worked hard for we struggled together to get where we are right now." Tamia answered.

"Yeah but Bourbon is right if it weren't for you I wouldn't be eating like I am right now. You are the one that found the wholesalers." Sanaa said as she thought about what Bourbon said starting to let her words get to her.

"Oh let me call the cops so they can fill out a report, I'll call my insurance company in the morning and have the car towed somewhere." Sanaa said as she pulled out her cell phone.

After she completed her call she just stared at Tamia.

"So what if I found the wholesalers, you know what we went through to open the shop up in the first place. We built that shop with our bare hands starting out doing hair in the kitchen, remember that? Remember what we went through after it opened when our clientele wasn't up, the guys we had to fuck to get money from to pay the bills at the shop? Huh? They don't know that but you do. Yeah I can open another shop up and survive on my own and so could you but that one has sentimental value. You've been riding and holding me down since day one so you have sentimental value to me now why would I give all of that up I would be a fool, you want them cut off they cut off." Tamia explained after taking in the events that happened so far that night.

"Look I think I should tell you something." Sanaa responded thinking this was the perfect moment.

She didn't notice the club had already let out and when she did she decided to wait.

"What? Tell me what?" Tamia asked anxious to know.

"I'll wait I don't want the whole club in our business it's bad enough they're seeing my car destroyed." Sanaa answered as she rolled her eyes at her once flawless Benz.

Bourbon, 2Cent, Redds, Shawna, and Shantel were growing restless watching from a distance because they couldn't hear anything. "We can pull off now I seen that bitch reaction I'm cool now." Bourbon said to the other two girls.

"No wait I want to see if that bitch catches a cab I would love to see that shit." 2Cent stopped Bourbon from starting the car.

"I would too." Redds added.

"Don't you see Tamia right there she's going to take her home." Bourbon said agitated.

When the police car finally pulled up Sanaa just wanted to give her statement and go home it's been a long night. She talked to the officer for about fifteen minutes before he gave her a police report number and pulled off.

"Damn I thought she was going to get the cop to take her home." 2Cent said.

"Wait a minute where is Tamia's Escalade at? I don't see it out here anywhere." Bourbon asked when the parking lots were almost empty.

"I don't know maybe it's around the corner." Redds replied.

"Nah look." Bourbon spoke as they watched Tamia and Sanaa get into the CLK they were all drooling over before they entered the club.

When Tamia pulled off she didn't notice the girls parked across the street nor did Sanaa.

"That sneaky bitch all that time we talking about that car in the club not once did she save us the embarrassment and say it was her car I feel like a nut." 2Cent angrily said.

"I know me too." Redds agreed. Shantel and Shawna exited their cars and walked over to Bourbon's Durango.

"Y'all see that shit I'm glad y'all ain't pull off yet see what I mean I know y'all down with us now because if we ain't know Tamia had that car then I know y'all ain't know because we always at the shop." Shantel said.

"No, we didn't know." Bourbon angrily responded.

"What's the plan y'all?" Redds asked also angry.

"Let's see if we can catch up so we can follow them they going to Sanaa's house I know they are we going to sit on these bitches for a while." Shawna answered like she had the plan figured out already.

Tamia stopped at the Wawa on Delaware Ave. before she got on the ramp to I95 South. This gave their enemies time to catch up.

"So what did you have to tell me Sanaa?" Tamia asked out of curiosity.

"Look Mia we been friends for years now and when we crossed the line and started pleasing each other sexually I started." Sanaa took a long pause before continuing.

Tamia pulled away from the Wawa still waiting for Sanaa to continue. The girls were coming through the light as they spotted Tamia turning onto the ramp.

"Just say it Sanaa, What is it? Tamia said wanting her to finish her sentence.

They rode in silence the whole ride until they got to the Claymont Exit in Delaware. When Tamia pulled in front of Sanaa's Apartment building in Green Tree Sanaa began to finish what she was saying.

"Mia I'm in love with you I been in love with you for years now any time somebody gets close to you I get jealous I don't want anybody taking you away from me I was jealous when you told me about Ice, I'm all the way now Mia I haven't been attracted to guys for three years now." Sanaa blurted out. Tamia was speechless.

"Say something Mia." Sanaa pleaded.

Tamia looked deep into her eyes before she leaned in to kiss her. They were so into the kiss they never noticed the cars pull up in the parking lot. After five minutes Tamia pulled away.

"Let's go upstairs." Tamia said seductively. They exited the car and did just that.

"Did y'all bitches see that shit these bitches is fucking each other." Redds said pointing out the obvious.

"So, this Bitch lives up here huh? All this long time I thought she still lived in the city. I can get her door kicked in while she at the shop. She don't know what she started and Tamia I know that bitch hustle she going to get hers too, I know she ain't stupid enough to keep anything at her spot so it's somewhere else and we need to find it she got paper that Benz had to cost some gwap to get customized, we going to set her ass up. My brother do stick ups we going to see what's what real soon." Bourbon said letting her jealousy and hate get the best of her.

CHAPTER FOUR:

CHAOS

Four months later, Fats and Flex sold so much cocaine and saved up so much money. That now they were ready to face Tamia to ask her the big question that they were plotting on all along.

Tamia was up to twenty five kilos a week. She didn't like how burned out she was becoming, juggling her marijuana business and her cocaine business along with her clientele at the shop. Things were getting hectic for her. Sometimes Sanaa would have to take her appointments for her leaving her stuck in the shop for six days instead of five and also working until one, two sometimes three in the morning. Tamia didn't like that at all especially with the beef between her and Bourbon, Redds, and 2Cent. Something had to give and it had to give fast. It would little did she know.

It was a very hot day the sun was starting to peak. Tamia was in route to meet her lieutenants when an alert came through her phone.

"What's up S? Tamia answered.

"Mia these bitches didn't show up today they didn't call or anything, I need you boo ASAP the shop is packed." Sanaa said in a panic like tone.

"Ok I'll be there in a little bit." Tamia answered.

"Shit, neither one of these bitches showed up huh what the fuck is that about?" She thought to herself.

Tamia thought about getting out of the cocaine business for good and handing everything over to Fats and Flex. She had already made her money and had a nice stash put away. When she finally reached the meeting spot Fats handed her the money both he and Flex owed her then he began to speak.

"Spazz look, I know you tired of bagging that shit up every week and me and Flex been stacking our money like crazy. What I'm asking from you is to give us the ok to take over the blocks now instead of running it for you. We buy the bricks from you and do it that way." Fats asked hesitantly.

"Do you think y'all ready for that?" Tamia asked. In the back of her mind she was happy they saved up enough money to buy their own kilos. She got her price knocked down to ten thousand dollars per kilo after she reached ten kilos so she was all for wholesaling.

"All right I'll charge y'all twenty thousand a brick until the number increase. All after that the price drops I'm only going to do this for a while then turn you on to the Connect. I'm almost done with this shit anyway." Tamia explained. They were happy to hear that and it showed.

"Look, after y'all knock off this work I got bagged up we can start. Oh and y'all niggas going to have to buy them blocks off me first and for most. I built most of them but the ones you opened are all yours I want fifty per block equaling two hundred and fifty thousand after you pay me that then you can buy your first bricks from me." Tamia said handing them their next package.

They weren't expecting her to say that but they had the money to pay her for the blocks so they agreed to it. Tamia then went to get all the bagged up cocaine she had and dropped it off to her two lieutenants then headed to the shop to help Sanaa.

When she finally made it to the shop she couldn't believe her eyes it was more packed in there than usual.

"These bitches picked the wrong day to not show up with all this money to be made in here today they could've increased their clientele." Tamia thought to herself as she started to put on her smock.

"Am I glad to see you Mia this has been the worst day of my life I'm exhausted already." Sanaa said.

"I got you S go take a break. I'll finish the ones under the dryer, and I called my two nieces to come in and be shampoo girls for the day. They should be here any minute we're going to get through this so relax I got some Patron waiting when we get done this crowd." Tamia reassured her.

Sanaa started to smile from ear to ear after she heard that. She hurried to the store to get a Red Bull and got right back to work. After a long day they finally got the crowd out the door. Tamia wanted to know what was going on.

"So tell me S did you have an argument with them or something?" Tamia asked trying to get to the bottom of the situation.

"Nothing new just about them asking for some of our clientele as usual but since I got you alone, someone broke in my house the other day I didn't get a chance to talk to you about it because of our busy schedules lately." Sanaa responded.

"Did they take anything?" Tamia asked.

"They took all my flat screens, computers, digital cameras, my fur and Gucci bags. Besides that they ransacked it probably looking for money or something, because if it was somebody that was watching me then they know I don't go to the bank. so they probably thought the money was at my spot." Sanaa answered.

"It probably was them bitches they probably followed you home and had someone break in your apartment. Bourbon, 2Cent, and Redds can be shiesty at times if that's how they playing then two can play that game." Tamia said thinking out loud.

"What do you have in mind?" Sanaa asked.

"First you're moving in with me for a while. I got my complex on lock so if anyone tries to break in they won't make it out if you know what I mean. We got cameras in this shop if they want to think they're coming up in here to take something the safe is in the floor and they definitely won't be smart enough to check that. Only you and I know it's there, my weed I'm taking that out of here tomorrow morning. I don't know if Shawna and Shantel had this shit done or Bourbon, 2Cent, and Redds but either way they all get it that way I know I got the right one, if it's one thing I can't stand is jealous bitches and stick up boys they on the same level as snitches if you ask me. Off the strength of me they should've left you alone but nobody fucks with my girl." Tamia answered.

"Okay Mia I'll move in with you but that's going to seem like I'm running don't you think? You taught me how to shoot at the gun range and I have a nine millimeter so what's the problem?" Sanaa asked as if she was ready for war.

"The problem is they hit your spot when you weren't there that means if they try it again they'll make sure your not home which means you'll never get a chance to use that gun. I have twenty four hour surveillance in my complex so your stuff will be safe. After this war is finished then we'll find you another apartment or we'll get a house together." Tamia responded.

"Well in that case where are we moving to?" Sanaa said with a smile as she pinched one of her nipples.

"Go ahead girl stop." Tamia said.

A few days had passed before Tamia got a phone call from Fats and Flex. They had the two hundred and fifty thousand to buy the blocks from her and the money from the rest of the bagged up product. When she went to pick the money up they put in an order for ten kilos and told her they need it by Friday. That gave Tamia a few days to re-up. She only had ten left and she knew those two were going to hit the ground running. But when she called Hector the bad news he gave her brought tears to her eyes. Carlos was murdered.

"Sorry for your loss Hec, I'm going to miss Carlos, when is the funeral?" She asked.

"It's Friday the funeral is Friday." Hector responded.

"Okay I'll definitely be there." Tamia responded.

"Okay well you can pick up your laundry before the viewing." Hector responded.

"Okay I'll see you then." Tamia said reading between the lines.

After she hung up with Hector she started to cry so uncontrollably that she had to pull over until she stopped crying.

"Damn what could happen next? Fuck, what the hell else can go wrong?" Tamia shouted out.

After she pulled herself together she pulled off. Carlos had West and South West Philly, Trenton and Camden on lock. Once Tamia got to the shop she called the Daily News and the Daily Times to put Help Wanted ads in both papers. Those positions were filled within two days of running the ads.

When Friday morning came Tamia got dressed to go to Carlos's funeral. When she met with Hector she rode with him to the funeral after they made the exchange.

"Spazz I need to know who did this they found him in Philly if you hear anything or find the guy or guys who did this I have twenty five bricks for you that was my baby cousin." Hector said with tears in his eyes.

"Say no more Hec I'll keep my ears open." Tamia responded.

They rode the rest of the ride in silence. After the burial Hector took Tamia back to her truck. She then went straight over the bridge to her stash house to weigh it then called the boys so they can pick up their order. Fats and Flex came to the house as usual except this time they weren't alone. They pulled up at the same time Tamia did. The car was tinted so Tamia never saw Shawna and Shantel in the back seat. Tamia got out of the car first then headed inside the house.

"That's y'all Boss?" Shawna asked.

"Was, she was our boss we our own bosses now we run Philly." Flex responded trying to impress his new play toy.

"Well we used to work for her too until y'all hooked us up with two chairs at your peeps barbershop and hair salon that Bitch own Spoiled Br@ Hair Technicians in Chester and she y'all connect now?" Shawna said digging for information.

"Flex I told you we should've dropped these bitches off, y'all better keep y'all mouths shut I don't like anybody in my business and neither do Spazz so don't assume what you don't know." Fats angrily interrupted as he shot a look of death at Flex.

"Come on dumb ass we're not suppose to mix business with pleasure remember if Spazz find out it was us that stole her workers we finished." Fats continued as he started to get out of the car.

Once the boys finally made it in the house Tamia rushed the transaction so she could hurry to the shop. Once the boys got back in the car they were attacked with questions by Shawna and Shantel.

"So y'all call her Spazz huh? Why y'all call her that? How long have y'all known her?" Shantel asked.

"What is this? Twenty one questions it's none of your business." Fats snapped at Shantel.

"You're already talking too much. I didn't even know she owned that shop and I probably wasn't supposed to know either. So you won't get anything out of me to go run your mouth to someone else." Fats continued to snap.

When Tamia got to the shop the two new stylists were already there and so was Sanaa. She had already shown them around the shop. Keisha was from Delaware and Amber was from Philadelphia. They were so easy going that even Sanaa got along with them. For Tamia that was the only good thing that was happening at the moment. A stressed Tamia asked Sanaa could she speak to her in private. Once they got in the office Sanaa already knew what she wanted by the look on Tamia's face.

So Sanaa started to give Tamia a massage to ease some of the tension. When they got five minutes into the massage they heard someone walk inside of the shop. Sanaa stopped to peep out and seen that there were a few walk in clients that came in.

"Are you girls ok or do you need some assistance?" Sanaa asked.

"No we're fine." The girls said in unison.

Sanaa then closed the door back and finished the massage.

"I already know Mia I can see that you're stressed out, maybe afterwards you can tell me what's on your mind." Sanaa said.

"I will, during our pillow talk though I don't feel like talking right now I just want to get this day over with." Tamia responded.

The news about their relationship was all over the city of Chester. They weren't exactly sure how it got out but they still denied it. When they came out of the office both of their appointments were walking in the door.

"Perfect timing, so what were you two bitches up to in there?" Keona asked smiling as if she knew something.

"Shut up girl and come over here so I can wash your hair." Tamia responded not really in the mood.

Keisha and Amber looked at each other wanting to know exactly what Keona meant by her question. When they saw Sanaa smiling devilishly they were curious to know what was up and what they were getting themselves into. Later on that night after they closed the shop and was long gone someone broke inside. The only thing that was missing was the Flat Screen everything else was just ransacked. Obviously they were looking for money. When Sanaa got to the shop the next morning she was devastated and called Tamia immediately. When Sanaa informed Tamia of the break in she wasted no time getting to the shop. Tamia went straight to the office and unlocked it. She saw where someone tried to break inside to no avail. Sanaa called the police and after she hung up Tamia grabbed her and held her until she stop crying. Tamia was happy she got the marijuana out of the shop. When the police came to fill out the report Tamia remembered the camera. She quickly went into the office to make a copy before she gave it to the officer while he was talking to Sanaa. She wanted a copy to review it herself so she could know what her next move would be. When the officer left, Sanaa's tears turned into anger as she started to vent out her frustrations.

"I know them bitches are behind this shit I want them dead Tamia and I'm not playing. Ain't nobody going to keep breaking into my shit I mean that if I have to go down there and do it myself I will." Sanaa angrily screamed out. "

Calm down Sanaa they are definitely going to get what they got coming. I promise you they playing with fire like they don't know I own half this shop. But that's if it's them so before you fly off the handle let's go look at the tape." Tamia said trying to calm Sanaa down.

At first when they looked at the tape they didn't recognize who it was. After they watched the tape over and over again Sanaa noticed some braids coming out of the person's skullcap and a tattoo that only Bourbon's brother Shawn had. Before she could say anything to Tamia, Keisha and Amber walked inside of the shop. They called out to the back where the office was. Tamia came out of the office to greet them.

"What happened?" Keisha asked.

"Hello ladies someone broke in last night but all they took was the TV and trashed the place." Tamia answered.

"Wow, do you want us to help clean up before clients start coming in?" Keisha asked.

"We're closed until Tuesday we need this place spotless before we can do hair and I need this window fixed first." Tamia answered.

"Okay well then we'll start picking up." Amber said adding to the conversation.

"Thank you Keisha, thank you Amber." Tamia said as she headed back into the office.

"That's Shawn Mia. I told you it was them bitches. Oh it's on now I'm calling my cousin he don't like Shawn either, oh he going to get his." Sanaa said shaking her head as if she was gesturing yes.

"No, look I want you to go to the police station and tell them who it was. Let them handle him I got something else for Bourbon." Tamia responded.

"What do you have in mind, Mia?" Sanaa asked with a grin on her face.

"A cocktail party of course, this should keep them busy for a while maybe they'll even come to their senses." Tamia answered.

"Okay Mia I like the way you think with bourbon's brother out of the way it'll be harder for them to retaliate." Sanaa said as a big smile came across her face.

"Go head to the police station while I help them clean this place up." Tamia said.

"Okay I'm out." Sanaa said as she exited the office and out the door.

A few days later Shawn was arrested under the charges of breaking and entering along with Robbery. Tamia threw her cocktail party that same night. The next day the shop was back open. With Sanaa going back and forth to court Tamia had to increase her hours at the shop. She had a lot more time on her hands than before because she didn't have to bag anything up she was literally buying and selling cocaine. As for her marijuana business that was always under control. Her life was a little calm now without all of the ripping and running Fats and Flex were putting her through. Yet she still needed a sit down with Hector.

Tamia never wanted to be this large in the drug game all she wanted and needed was the money. Now she was knee deep into it and wanted out. The only thing she wanted at this point was to run the shop. Tamia had other things she was planning to do with herself. She had dreams of becoming a Rapper under her own record label, she wanted to put out a clothing line open a chain of restaurants and start a chain of beauty salons. The drug game was never for her. She needed out and she wanted out before her long run in the business ended with her behind bars or in a tragic death. She called Hector to arrange a meeting at the end of the week.

In the mean time she would sell the rest of the cocaine she had to Fats and Flex. When Sunday came she was prepared to face Hector with the dilemma she had. When she walked into the office at Hector's club he knew something was wrong by the look on her face.

"What is it Spazz? You look like you are afraid to tell me what it is that you have to say. Did you take a loss and need to be fronted or something? Or did you find Carlos's killer and it's someone you know?" Hector asked.

"It's neither one, look I've been dealing with you for years now and I'm growing tired of this game I want out and I was wondering if I can turn my two lieutenants on to you so they can continue. I mean I've been wholesaling to them for a while now they're ready to step up to the challenge." Tamia answered.

"Well Spazz you know all money ain't good money. I trust very few people but if you're vouching for them I'm going to go out on a limb and do you this favor we can arrange a meeting tomorrow if you'd like." Hector responded.

That was music to Tamia's ears.

"Okay Hec thanks I'll set it up." Tamia said happily.

"No need to thank me I thought you were too pretty to be out here doing this anyway you should pursue a modeling career or something I really think that you are so beautiful." Hector said as he stood up to walk Tamia to the door.

Thank you Hector I appreciate this I'm going to pursue a fashion career I want to put out a clothing line I'll design you a whole wardrobe to show you my appreciation I'll see you tomorrow." Tamia said as she started to walk towards the door.

"Okay Spazz good luck with that clothing line." Hector responded.

Tamia called Fats to arrange a meeting as soon as she walked out of the club. She wanted to tell them in person. When she got to them she noticed that they were acting a little funny but she disregarded it. When she told them the news they were happier than a kid in a candy store.

"I told you Flex I told you those all nighters were going to pay off all right Spazz thanks we'll see you tomorrow." Fats responded to the news.

Tamia couldn't wait to tell Sanaa so she called her to tell her she was on her way home. First she stopped pass Naaman's Beverage to pick up a few bottles of Moet because this was a cause for a celebration. When Tamia got home with the bottles of Champagne Sanaa was all smiles because she already knew what was in the bag. She took the bag out of Tamia's hands and took it in the kitchen.

"So what are we celebrating Mia?" Sanaa asked.

"Well for starters I wanted to say you've been riding with me for years now, and I appreciate everything you put up with during those times. You had to hold the shop down when I was out taking care of business. Secondly, I know you've been wanting me to get out of the streets for some time now, and I want to tell you that I'm finally out. I'm out of the dope game for good. Now I have to slowly get out of the weed game and I'm officially out of the streets now I can spend more time with you at the shop and here at the house because my weed clientele doesn't keep me ripping and running." Tamia let out her good news. Sanaa started to squeal with joy.

"Are you serious you're done for real?" Sanaa asked.

"Yes and guess what else I'm going to start on the clothing line. I want to put on our first fashion show at the beginning of next year are you with me." Tamia asked giving her part three of what she had to tell her.

"Of course I'm with you Mia I been riding with you for this long why wouldn't I be, this is a reason to celebrate." Sanaa responded as she popped one of the bottles and poured two glasses.

"Okay let's toast partners until the end?" Tamia asked.

"To us being partners until the end." Sanaa responded as they clanged glasses and drank to their new beginning.

On Tuesday they gave the girls the news about the fashion show.

"Ooh I can't wait." Amber said with excitement.

"Me either." Keisha added also excited.

"So you girls think you can hang with the big dogs for this fashion show I mean we are the top two stylists in the Tri-State?" Tamia asked jokingly.

"Oh we can hang." Keisha responded.

"Yeah we can hang. You two bitches might be famous for doing hair and made history with this shop because it's the only one that sells weave. But don't sleep on us we can do some hair now don't get it twisted. Tamia you two did not hire some slouches remember that." Amber added.

"Well all right we'll see." Tamia responded.

CHAPTER FIVE:

RIVERSIDE REVENGE

Hutch was up to buying twenty five pounds and Starsky was at twenty. The two partners had the Riverside Projects on lock and half of Wilmington, Delaware. They were the stars of the city. Hutch always was very popular with the ladies he stood at six foot three inches tall with a muscular frame caramel complexion and hazel eyes. Every girl already wanted Hutch but with his status in the game that increased. His sidekick on the other hand was just the opposite. The money made the girls flock after him.

Starsky was black as night with crooked teeth and a bad over bite. When he smiled he tried not to show his teeth because of that and with all the money he was making you'd think he would get his teeth fixed.

They were nicknamed Starsky and Hutch from the movie because they were always together. They were on top and feeling real good about themselves so they decided to throw a party at A Club Called West open bar. West didn't mind since they gave him two thousand to rent out the club for the night.

The party was one party the city of Wilmington would never forget. They had male strippers, female strippers, and bottles popping. Everyone had a ball courtesy of Starsky and Hutch. They were having the time of their lives until the club let out. What Starsky and Hutch didn't realize was that Juice came home from prison two weeks prior to the party. He had the whole Riverside on lock before he was sentenced to ten years. He came home with a vengeance because he wanted his Project back.

Shots rapidly rang out as the club was emptying out. Some scattered while others dove to the ground. After Juice sped off the ones that were on the ground noticed that someone was lying on the ground squirming as they were getting up.

"Yo Hutch, Starsky hit son." One of the party goers yelled out. Hutch ran over to him.

"Yo help me get him in the car fuck the ambulance he won't make it if we wait on them he lost too much blood." Hutch yelled back to the party goer.

"Yo Hutch I'm not going to make it son take care of my daughter for me can you promise me that?" Starsky asked as Hutch started to get him off the ground.

"Stop talking like that you going to be here to do it yourself you going to make it I got you." Hutch responded hoping he was right.

"If I don't do you promise?" Starsky asked.

"I'm her godfather ain't I? You know I'm going hold you down but you better hold on nigga. You're all I got hold on we're almost there." Hutch responded.

Starsky had been shot in the neck, stomach arm and leg. When they finally made it to the emergency room Starsky passed out. Hutch had to do a lot of screaming and yelling before they bought out a gurney to take him into an operating room. After about twelve hours of fighting the machine Starsky was hooked up to went to a flat line. When the doctor came out Hutch burst into tears he had already knew he was gone the moment the machine went to a flat line. He was so close to Starsky he felt everything. He always knew when something was wrong with his lifetime partner in crime. The doctor broke the news to the family and they were hysterical.

"Hutch, how could you let this happen to my baby?" Starsky's mother screamed as she started beating on his chest.

He just stood there taking every punch. He felt her pain. She had just lost her child and he had just lost his only friend. When she finished hitting him Hutch stood there holding her until she pulled herself together.

Hutch was devastated he didn't know what to do next his body went numb. He never thought this day would come any time soon.

"We didn't have any enemies so who could've shot our party up? Was that meant for me am I next?" Hutch thought to himself.

For the next two days he stayed in the house mourning his best friend. He wasn't eating anything just smoking marijuana back to back for two whole days until he got a phone call from his cousin Eric.

"Hello." Hutch answered.

"Yo Hutch did you know that nigga Juice home? My man Maine said that nigga started snapping when he found out y'all was running Riverside now and half of Wilmington he said Juice was the one that shot the party up and you next so when we suiting up?" Eric asked with vengeance in his voice.

Hutch was shocked. The same guy that used to run Starsky and Hutch off the block when they were fifteen just killed his partner.

"We suiting up tonight bring me a bottle of Henny." Hutch responded.

When he hung up the phone he threw the remote to the television at the wall across the room.

"How the fuck this nigga going to think he can come home after ten years and pick up where he left off. After ten fucking years? Kill my man, and now threaten my life over some shit he thinks belong to him that's my project now." He snapped.

After he lit up another Dutch Master filled with marijuana he realized he was talking to himself. Later that night Eric showed up to Hutch's house.

"What's up Hutch where we going to go look for this nigga at I don't know where he stay at." Eric asked.

"I don't know man you got that Henny for me." Hutch asked.

"Yeah man but what's the plan." Eric responded.

"It ain't a plan we just going to ride around until we find that nigga that's it shoot on sight." Hutch responded.

"All right if you say so let's go." Eric responded not really liking the plan.

As soon as they stepped outside the house they heard shots one of them zipped pass Hutch's ear they almost fell over each other trying to get back inside.

Unlike Hutch and Eric, Juice had a plan. The party was so well promoted that he knew exactly where Starsky and Hutch would be that night. Only he thought he was going to get a chance to kill them both. It was all over the jail when Juice was incarcerated that Starsky and Hutch was running things in Riverside and half of Wilmington. Juice had to hear about this for his last five years in prison. All he did was gather information about the two friends while he was in prison so he could know everywhere he could find them. He had five years of anger built up and he was releasing it on Starsky and Hutch.

"Fuck, that nigga outside let's go out the back door." Hutch angrily suggested.

By the time they made it around to the front Juice was already pulling off.

"Yo hurry up we got to catch up to this nigga." Hutch said as he ran to his car.

After Eric got in they sped off after him spotting him two lights up on Governor Printz.

"It's now or never cousin catch that nigga." Eric said as he cocked his .50 Caliber.

As soon as Hutch was about to floor it he spotted two police cars turning on to Governor Printz responding to the call of shots being fired in Riverside. He slowed down and Juice got away. They were upset about missing their chance to kill Juice they decided to stay in a hotel in case he came back.

The next morning Hutch went over to Starsky's mom house to give her some money for the funeral and to help make arrangements he even volunteered to be a pallbearer. Before he left he told her he would pick out and pay for Starsky's suit he wanted him to be buried in. He wanted to send his best friend home in style. He went to Man's World in the

Tri-State Mall the next day to get it. He never bothered to tell her he knew who the shooter was because he had already decided he was going to revenge his best friend's death so he kept it to himself.

The day of the funeral something didn't set right with Hutch but he ignored the feeling. After the service started that feeling came back but even stronger.

"Something's not right." Hutch thought to himself.

He sat through the service trying to shake the feeling but couldn't. He got up to help carry the casket. The moment they walked outside the church. The pallbearers were shot at.

"This disrespectful motherfucker I guess this was the bad feeling I couldn't shake. Oh this nigga is really out of hand now." Hutch thought to himself.

"Somebody call the ambulance." Starsky's mom yelled out.

One of Starsky's brothers was shot in the leg and his father was shot in the shoulder. Hutch had his mind made up that when he finally caught Juice his funeral would be closed casket.

"I'll wait for the Ambulance you go and bury your son ma'am." One of the Deacons said.

"Okay thank you Deacon." Starsky's mother responded.

They went to the graveyard to finish the ceremony. Hutch was very emotional. He felt angry, sad and hurt all at the same time. He knew it had to happen soon or more people were going to get hurt or killed because of this lunatic. After the words ashes to ashes and dust to dust left out of the pastor's mouth. More shots rang out. Juice was on a rampage. The only thing that could stop him was either him taking a bullet or Hutch dead. After the shooting they finished the burial luckily no one was injured Hutch and Eric went home to change. They decided it was time to look for Juice. They wouldn't rest until Juice was dead.

"This is the ultimate disrespect, this nigga shot up Starsky's funeral twice in one day, almost shot me in front if my own door." Hutch thought to himself.

He was on a mission that would result in someone residing in a grave. He planned to tear Wilmington up looking for Juice. He decided to start at the root of the problem. Riverside Projects to ask around about where he was staying. After asking around for a few days no one knew anything. His family moved out of the project a few years back and no one knew exactly where they just knew in a house on the other side of Wilmington. Hutch decided to go over there to ask around but still no answers. Juice was only known in the projects and around that area no one knew Juice on the other side of Philadelphia Pike. That part of Wilmington he could lay low without having to worry. The more he asked around the angrier he became with coming up empty.

"Damn this is stopping my money, Eric I need this nigga dead ASAP." Hutch screamed out of frustration.

Meanwhile, they were looking for Juice and he was at the 211 Lounge in Claymont getting drunk. The bar was almost empty there were only two other people inside besides Juice and the bar maid. Juice knew Hutch wouldn't be able to find him there because he only hung in A Club Called West and Pharaoh's. Anywhere else he frequent was in Philly.

While Juice was out in Claymont he noticed it was money in that area so he decided to set up shop out in Claymont until he got his project back then he'd have both cities on lock. Juice had big plans for the state of Delaware and planning on getting Hutch out of the picture was one of them. He was upset he missed three times he knew Hutch already knew what time it was by now. He needed to plan his next attack on him.

Hutch decided it was time to change the plan instead of riding around in search of Juice he'd make Juice come to him. From that day forward shop was open only now Hutch was on frontline with a bullet proof vest on and two nine millimeters on him. The project was famous for so much violence the police would never patrol through there. They only went to that project when they were called.

After about a week on the frontline Hutch actually started to think Juice wasn't coming. But no way was he going to let his guard down he was sad that he was making money without his deceased partner but vowed to always make sure Wilmington remembers Starsky. He talked to his cousin earlier that day to have a memorial drawn in the middle of the project. He wanted his face and some angel wings coming from his back with the born and death dates underneath. In the back of his mind he hoped Juice didn't destroy it.

A week later it was spray painted. Everyone started lighting candles for Starsky putting flowers in front of the memorial along with teddy bears. When Hutch seen that he couldn't help but to smile as a tear came down his face. The next day he went to the tattoo parlor to get a tear drop tatted on his face like Baby from Cash Money. On his forearm he got Starsky's picture with R.I.P under it.

Still no sign of Juice he was in Claymont building his clientele. He even rented out an apartment. Everything was going fine for him his connect always had in some good marijuana so he was loving life at the moment. When he got to twenty pounds he would plan another attack on Hutch and take over the project.

Hutch continued to stay on the frontline even though there's been no sign of Juice he still stayed on his p's and q's knowing Juice could pop up at any minute. Riverside was popping again only this time he didn't have his side kick with him. Eric was doing a good job of filling Starsky's shoes but it still wasn't the same without him. Hutch planned on taking his and Starsky's daughter to Six Flags the next day. Neither of the girls could get enough of the amusement park. He gave Starky's daughters' mother some money he had been saving to open up a savings account and to get her some savings bonds when he went to pick her up.

Meanwhile Juice was having the time of his life in Claymont. He decided to go to Delilah's to watch the strippers dance. He was feeling himself at the moment because he was up to five pounds and felt like he was on a rise back to the top. He ran into his Chester and Philly associates in Delilah's. Juice felt like he was getting back connected again making plans to put some cocaine in Claymont along with his marijuana. He figured he would have Claymont on lock down enough to attack Hutch and make a killing in the project. There's one thing he knew about fiends they embrace anybody with a good product. He'd have his project back in no time. Just as soon as he got rid of Hutch, but what Juice didn't know was Hutch was planning on killing him and keeping his project. Hutch isn't the same young kid he used to run off the strip before he went to jail for ten years Hutch was ready for war.

Everyone was there to see Diamond dance she was the top stripper in Philadelphia. She was five foot six inches tall pretty face red bone with nice breast and a round butt. As Juice was leaving Delilah's he was too drunk to notice someone from Riverside in the crowd on the outside. He was occupied by two bi- sexual females that wanted to play with him that night. He felt like he was on top of the world his manhood was rock hard and he had not one but two females. He thought of the cheapest hotel in the area the Motel 7 in Essington. He'd have fun with the girls and take them home in the morning. One of Hutch's runners got in his car and followed them. He lingered back to see what room they were going into. After all three went inside he immediately called Hutch to give him the information. As soon as he received the news Hutch was happier than ever so he called Eric.

"Hello." Eric answer.

"Yo E my young buck found this nigga he at the Motel 7 in Essington let's go end this nigga career." Hutch happily said.

"All right." Eric answered before hanging up the phone.

When they got to the hotel they decided to wait to see if Juice or one of the girls were going to come out to get ice. They were hoping they weren't going to have to wait until he checked out.

"Hutch didn't your young buck say he was with two girls you know that nigga ain't going to smash and leave we're going to be here until he checks out." Eric said.

"So what, that disrespectful motherfucker got to pay so we waiting."
Hutch responded angrily.

"Okay, if you say so." Eric responded.

Meanwhile Juice was inside having the time of his life it was his first
threesome. He hadn't been with a woman in ten years.

"What a welcome home present." He thought to himself.

After he finished playing with the girls they fell asleep. Juice woke
up first and got in the shower. When the girls heard Juice in the shower
they were awaken from their sleep. The first thing the girls did was start
playing with each other that wasn't anything new for them. That's what
they did every morning. When Juice came out of the bathroom he got an
instant hard on seeing the girls going at each other. He wasted no time
joining in stamina wasn't a problem for him. When they got finished all
three took a shower together. Feeling like a new man now he was ready
to get back to Claymont to get more money.

As soon as they started to leave the room, Hutch opened fire on
them. Juice was shot in the arm, one of the girls was shot in the leg, and
the other girl made it to the ground without getting hit by a bullet. Juice
ran for cover and started returning shots. He hit Eric in the chest and
Hutch in the neck and took off running. He saw an older couple getting
in to their cars and jacked them for it then headed to I95 South back to
Claymont leaving the two girls there.

Hutch rushed Eric to the hospital and once he got there he collapsed.
Both of them were in the emergency room right next to each other.
Hutch struggled to survive but he finally pulled through after a few
hours went by. The bullet pierced his lung so the doctors had to remove
it.

Eric on the other hand didn't make it the bullet was too close to his
heart for them to get it out without doing any damage to it. This was

the second funeral in a matter of three months Hutch was feeling worst than ever. He wanted Juice dead and wouldn't rest until he was. After thinking about it he was mad at himself for not getting Juice when he had the chance now his cousin is dead along with his best friend.

When Juice got back to Claymont he realized the bullet only grazed his arm so there was no need to go to the emergency room so he cleaned and bandaged it. He was angry he didn't get a chance to make sure Hutch was dead or had a number for one or both of the girls.

After that shoot out they didn't want to hear anyone mention the name Juice. One of the cops had to take the girl home that didn't get shot. The other one rode to Taylor Hospital in an Ambulance for treatment. Juice decided to pay Riverside a little visit to see if Hutch was dead or not. After asking a younger guy what he knew he slid him a hundred dollar bill and told him they never had the conversation. He was upset to find out that Hutch was still alive so he decided to lay low for a while. When he went back to Claymont he only came outside to serve his fiends. He needed an effective plan that would finish Hutch off for good.

The doctor wouldn't let Hutch leave the hospital until he was completely healed. He was upset but he had female visitors to help ease the pain. After Hutch left the hospital he was right back at it in the heart of the project hoping to bring Juice to him. No one had seen or heard from Juice while Hutch was in the hospital except for the younger guy Juice paid not to say anything. Hutch was growing tired of waiting. He had a little small beef but nothing this major the whole time he was hustling. This whole situation took Hutch by surprise but still he had to man up, after all the streets were watching and talking. He needed to end this war and end it fast.

Hutch was no gangster he was just a hustler. But if he let Juice punk him everyone would think he was soft and try him the same way and Hutch wasn't having that at all.

CHAPTER SIX:

THE PLOT THICKENS

Shantel and Shawna couldn't wait to get to Chester they had some news Bourbon, 2Cent, and Redds could use, well so they thought. They met with them at Binn's bar.

"Where the fuck y'all bitches been at y'all was in the wind when all the shit hit the fan what the fuck y'all bitches got to tell us and it better be good." Bourbon snapped.

"Well for starters we were at Palmer's and we ran into these fine ass Philly niggaz right." Shawna began.

"Wait, wait you mean to tell me y'all bitches were out getting some dick while all this shit was going on." Bourbon interrupted.

"Look let me finish do you want to hear the news or not." Shawna snapped back.

"Yeah we want to hear it go ahead." 2Cent answered for Bourbon.

"Well anyway they were flossing hard iced out and everything with some Red Monkey Jeans on both of them and a fly ass shirt you know cost some gwap. So we hook up with them and after kicking it with them for a month, one morning they was about to bring us back to Chester when their connect called and told them to meet her at their spot in twenty minutes so they didn't have a choice they had to take us. We pulled up at the same time she was pulling up. She got out the truck and walked in the house while we were parking and guess who the bitch was?" Shawna asked getting out what she had to say.

"Who was it?" Redds asked anxiously.

"That bitch Tamia you hear me they call this bitch Spazz can you believe that shit I thought the niggas worked for her but they said no we used to work for her they said we bosses now she our connect we run Philly y'all fucking with the Street Bosses of Philly sweethearts like that right, so I said she must be pushing major weight to be supplying y'all if y'all run Philly. So they said yeah but we put her on the map up here she got a good ass connect that's the only reason she our connect other than that they would be holding as many bricks as Ms. Tamia a.k.a Spazz you was right that Benz did cost some gwap to get customized she holding like a motherfucker we need to rob her ass tell your brother to sit on this bitch I remember where the house at she met them at too." Shawna said proud of the exaggerated news she just gave acting like she was ready for a medal of honor or something.

"Bitch that's what the fuck I been trying to tell you my brother got locked up for breaking into these bitches shop and Sanaa's apartment they just got finished going to court he got a three to six but that's not the half of it these bitches blew my car up, Redds car, and 2Cent house she live with me and my peoples now and I'm borrowing peoples whips cause I didn't have insurance." Bourbon snapped.

"My boyfriend got locked up for serving an undercover so he can't do it either." Redds added.

"My brother got shot from some beef he in so he can't do it." 2cent added.

"Well why we can't do it ourselves." Shantel asked.

"Well because I'm sure if she's holding all like that, she carries a gun and don't any of us have one." Bourbon said upset she even got involved in this to begin with let alone getting her brother involved she wanted to call a truce but was too stubborn to do it.

"So what are we going to do?" Shantel asked.

"Right now I don't know but if y'all come up with something let us know, Can I have an absolute and cranberry?" Bourbon responded as she ordered herself a drink.

"It seems like y'all are the ones that talked us into this shit and nothing happened to either one of y'all but something happened to each one of us. Sanaa moved in with Tamia now and from hanging with her I know somebody watches her spot. As for this house who's to say something is in there or not it could be somewhere else and I don't know any one else to rob her. I don't want any more family members locked up so y'all find somebody to do it." Bourbon continued after she took a sip of her drink.

Shawna and Shantel hadn't planned for that they thought this was in the bag.

"Well did y'all get anything from Sanaa's apartment or the shop?" Shantel asked.

"Yeah a couple of Flat Screens that's it." Bourbon lied she hadn't planned on giving those two anything from those robberies.

"Well we'll get back to you on a plan we'll be in touch y'all." Shawna said as her and Shantel left the bar.

"Look Shawna I think we should hit that house and say fuck them three bitches. Because I know they got more than that Tamia is paid and so is that bitch Sanaa. I mean we witnessed for ourselves how much money they bring in at the shop. On top of Tamia's hustle and I know she look out for Sanaa shit she probably brought her that CLS 500 in the first place. I'm thinking Sanaa was eating more and it was Tamia the whole time I need some of that money, How about you?" Shantel asked after giving her opinion on the situation.

"Yeah I'm with you." Shawna answered.

Later on that night they broke into the house Fats and Flex took them to and the only thing they found was a triple beam scale and a table with some chairs other than that the house was empty. They were highly upset.

"Bourbon was right it ain't shit in here I feel like a fool." Shawna said.

"Well where the fuck is her shit at?" Shantel asked frustrated.

"We need to follow this bitch everywhere she go. She'll lead us to something some money, some bricks something." Shawna responded.

"You right let's go to the shop and wait for them to close tomorrow they probably gone by now." Shantel said.

"Yeah they probably are." Shawna added.

Meanwhile after Ginn's closed Bourbon and her two friends were looking for some marijuana to smoke before they went in so by the time Shantel and Shawna made it back to Chester they ran into Bourbon, 2Cent, and Redds at the CITGO they were all there getting Dutch Masters to roll their marijuana up.

"Look at these bitches I don't believe they thought we were going to break them off after they got in the wind on us I'm done with them bitches." Bourbon said after she spotted Shantel and Shawna.

"Yeah me too." 2Cent and Redds said in unison.

"What's up Shawna?" Bourbon spoke.

"What's up with y'all?" Shawna responded.

"Getting ready to get a session going, where y'all coming from?" Bourbon asked making small talk while waiting in line.

"We coming from up top seeing them Philly niggaz I was telling you about and they said they just meet there that ain't her stash house you was right ain't shit there we just going to fall back on them they ain't slipping like I thought they were." Shawna answered.

"All right well we going to fall back too I'll hit y'all up later." Bourbon said as she headed back to the car.

"Them bitches must have hit that house and ain't find nothing I ain't got that them niggaz told them that it wasn't nothing in there that's what the fuck they get." Bourbon said as she got back inside the car.

"Is that what that bitch said." 2Cent asked.

"Yeah that's what that bitch said." Bourbon responded as she started to roll the marijuana up inside the Dutch Master.

After the girls finished smoking they went in the house same routine day in and day out. Get off work smoke, eat, smoke again, take a nap, smoke again, go to the bar leave there, smoke again then go to sleep and wake up and do it all over again. The next night Shantel and Shawna waited outside the shop to follow Tamia and Sanaa home but just their luck they went out to a club after they left the shop so they didn't get to find out where Tamia lived until a week later.

"Ballingford Estates huh all the money this bitch make and she live in Ballingford Estates I understand she might want to keep a low profile but where is the CLK I don't see it out here I wanted to steal it and take it to the shop chop." Shawna said.

"Yeah me too." Shantel agreed.

"I wonder what's in the apartment do she have any money or bricks in there or is it somewhere else." Shawna thought aloud.

"It might be in there the only way to find out is to go inside and take a look but since we know where she live let's wait to see if she goes to another house or something if we can get money and dope why not take it all." Shantel suggested.

They waited for a month and there was no sign of a stash house. What Shantel and Shawna didn't know was Tamia had left Spazz her street persona behind her it was too late for them to try to rob her. She introduced Fats and Flex to her cocaine connection and walked away.

Hutch and Juice was still beefing and Starsky was dead so her marijuana business was slow. They were her main customers. The only places they followed her to were the shop and home and the places they frequent to let their hair down. They were so upset and tired of waiting they decided to break in the apartment anyway despite Bourbon telling them someone watches the house. They made it inside the apartment and was so amazed at how well decorated it was. They didn't find any money but anything their heart desired as far as technology was concern. So they started helping themselves.

As soon as they walked out the door they were both killed. Their deaths made the Daily Times the heading read:

"Neighbor Hero during Burglary"

When Bourbon opened the paper she immediately called 2Cent and Redds to tell them to come over her house ASAP. When they arrived Bourbon said her famous line.

"We need to smoke this one over." They went to the waterfront to smoke once the Dutch was lit she opened the newspaper.

"Read this shit y'all." Bourbon said as she sparked up another Dutch.

After both girls read the article they were speechless for five minutes.

"Damn these bitches made the front page huh that's crazy." 2Cent broke the silence.

"That is crazy." Redds added.

"I guess they thought I was bullshitting when I said somebody watches her house or something that's what the fuck they get for being so hardheaded." Bourbon said in a hyper tone.

"I'm glad we did not keep fucking with them two bitches or we probably would be in this article." Redds added.

"Shit, no the fuck we wouldn't we already knew what time it was I tried to tell them bitches but they ain't listen." Bourbon angrily responded.

"Yeah you right." Redds responded.

"Y'all got some more weed?" Bourbon asked as she threw out the roach she was smoking.

"I don't but how much do you think Tamia paid her neighbor for that?" Redds asked.

"Probably like fifty thousand." 2Cent replied.

"I wonder what that bitch sitting on if she's pushing bricks." Bourbon said thinking aloud.

"I don't know but I kind of miss Tamia." 2Cent added.

"Well call her so that bitch can hang up in your ear dummy she chose that bitch over us so I say fuck her." Bourbon angrily responded.

"Bitch like you never left us hanging for some dick you need to stop and I'm starting to miss her too." Redds added.

"Well y'all can go back and hang with that bitch then but I don't fuck with Sanaa so as long as she in the picture I don't fuck with Tamia either." Bourbon snapped back being her usual stubborn self.

"Well you ain't got to I'm going to call her I just ain't got to fuck with Sanaa." 2Cent snapped back.

"Yeah but didn't Sanaa say she didn't want nobody around her pussy the last time we seen her at the club." Bourbon asked.

"Yeah, so what, fuck her I ain't scared of that bitch." Redds snapped.

"All right well, just don't call me to hang with y'all bitches. I'm tired of Sanaa and her insults." Bourbon said surrendering the argument.

"All right somebody roll up, arguing with you blew my high and are you going to the party at Club West Saturday? 2Cent asked changing the subject.

"Who party is it?" Redds asked.

"Ron is having it from the East Side." 2cent responded.

"Yeah I'm going I need to run into a Delaware sucker it ain't no more suckers in Chester." Bourbon added.

"Yeah I hear that." Redds added.

"I wonder if Tamia think Shantel and Shawna was in on the other two robberies with us." Redds asked.

"Yeah I forgot about that I ain't going to call her." 2Cent answered.

"Are y'all going to the funeral?" Redds asked.

"I might go to the viewing." Bourbon answered.

"I don't know if I'm going yet." 2Cent added.

"Is the weed gone?" Bourbon asked.

"Yeah it's gone." Redds answered.

"Alright I'm about to go to the crib and take a nap." Bourbon responded.

Bourbon didn't want to sit around anyone unless there was a Dutch burning. When the funeral for the girls came around both of them were closed casket. Everyone was shocked to see Sanaa and Tamia walk through the door. All you heard were whispers.

"What are they doing here didn't they try to rob one of them girl." A voice said from one of the pews.

"They used to work for them too." Another girl whispered.

"Why can't people just mind their fucking business?" Sanaa whispered to Tamia.

"I don't know but stop cursing in the church this funeral is packed I know it's a double funeral but these two conniving chicks had this many friends." Tamia replied.

"You see Redds and 2Cent over there I wonder why Bourbon didn't come." Sanaa whispered.

"They probably sent these bitches to your spot in the first place Mia see how slimy your old friends are? That's why I never wanted you around them." Sanaa continued.

"You don't know that Sanaa anyway we here let's talk about this after the burial ok." Tamia responded.

"Okay Mia." Sanaa answered.

After the funeral 2Cent and Redds went straight to Bourbon's house to talk about who was at the funeral.

"You know these bitches had a nerve to show up at the funeral." 2Cent started the conversation.

"Who showed up?" Bourbon asked.

"Bitch, Sanaa and Tamia them bitches is bold." Redds added.

"I told you they was probably going to show up that's why I only went to the viewing." Bourbon responded.

"Yeah but they didn't say anything to us so they probably wouldn't have said anything to you." 2Cent said.

"Well we out we going to the mall." Redds said as they got up to leave out.

"All right y'all I'm about to take a nap." Bourbon responded as she walked them out.

CHAPTER SEVEN:

BOTH SIDES

It was seven o'clock in the morning when Tamia was awaken by an alert.

"Everyday I'm hustling, Everyday I'm hustling." sang through the speakers of her phone until she answered.

"Yizzo" Tamia answered.

"What's up Spazz?" A familiar voice came through the speaker.

"What's up nigga, what time is it?" Tamia asked.

"It's seven o'clock." The familiar voice answered.

"Why so early tell me that what you want boy?" Tamia asked.

"Ten if you can wake up from your beauty sleep to come meet me I'll come to Chester if I have to." The voice responded.

"You have to now meet me down the way in twenty minutes." Tamia said.

"All right cool" the voice responded.

"What the fuck this nigga doing up at the crack of dawn for, I like money like the next person but damn seven in the morning. She got up to meet with him then came right back home to get in the bed. As soon as she went to sleep Sanaa woke her right back up. Sanaa woke up when Tamia came back to lie down.

"What are you doing up?" Tamia asked.

"I woke up horny so I decided to play with you are you mad at me?" Sanaa asked.

"How can I be mad being waken up like this if you keep this up I might have to take you shopping." Tamia said playfully.

"Well in that case." Sanaa responded as she proceeded like this was the last time she was going to have sex ever again.

She made her explode all over the bed a sight a straight guy would spend his last dollar to witness in person two drop dead gorgeous females pleasing each other.

"I love you Tamia." Sanaa said.

Instead of saying it back Tamia just looked in her eyes and returned the favor being the strong silent type that she is. Sanaa took the hint as they continued to please each other for the rest of the morning. They both went to the shop with big smiles on their faces. Everyone wanted to know why. They heard the rumors about the two friends but never picked up on any body language that confirmed the rumors as being true. That's the way they wanted to keep it the less people in their business the better for their relationship.

"Everyday I'm hustling, everyday I'm hustling" Tamia received another alert.

"Yizzo" She answered.

"Damn hotline." Sanaa said playfully.

"Spazz I need five more baby girl it's popping around here." The voice said.

"Yeah all right meet me at the spot in an hour and a half you got to come to Chester." Tamia responded.

"No problem" the voice responded back.

Tamia finished her clients before she left.

"I'll be back Sanaa can you take her from under the dryer for me if I'm not back in time." Tamia asked.

"Of course I will" Sanaa answered with a smile on her face.

It took Tamia twenty minutes to get those five pounds and meet with her customer.

"Look Juice, I ain't got time to count this I'm in a hurry but I will count it so it better be right." Tamia said sternly.

"It is, you got the best weed around now why would I fuck that up when I'm trying to take over the state I mean shit I'm back on the bricks now I'm hitting the ground running." Juice said with confidence.

"Yeah well don't get yourself into trouble and get sent back how's your arm." Tamia asked.

"It's cool" Juice responded.

"How did you get shot anyway?" Tamia asked.

"Some nigga that I owe a hot one to shot at me but it ain't about nothing though." Juice responded.

"Okay, I'm only looking out because you cool with my cousin. If you get popped don't expect me to look out when you get out, because I'm about to be done with this shit soon. So I won't be able to put you back on your feet when you come home so stay home and stay out of trouble." Tamia responded as she left to go back to the shop.

"So what kind of clothes are you designing Tamia?" Keisha asked.

"Yeah Tamia I can't wait for the fashion show so I can show off my skills." Amber added.

"I know that's right" added Sanaa.

"I'm designing everything from sportswear to suits and ties for the guys, and everything from sportswear to wedding gowns for the ladies. But y'all just make sure y'all get those styles right so they can bring out my designs. That's all y'all need to worry about." Tamia responded.

"Oh we got our end Ms. Thang." Keisha said as she snapped her finger.

"I'm hungry somebody order something." Sanaa said.

Right after the words left her mouth the door to the shop opened. When Tamia saw who it was that walked through the door her bottom lip dropped. Sanaa froze when she saw who it was. Keisha and Amber looked at one another after they saw Tamia and Sanaa's reactions. They couldn't believe their eyes. Tamia and Sanaa knew exactly who he was but Keisha and Amber on the other hand just laid eyes on the sexiest man they ever seen up close and personal. Derrick was finally home after doing eight years in the penitentiary on the other side of Pennsylvania. He was home and ready to claim what he felt was his wifey Ms. Tamia.

Derrick was the one who introduced Tamia to the cocaine business.

She was only selling Marijuana when he met her. He also got her connected with Hector. Derrick taught Tamia the rules to the game and how to present herself like a soldier and a boss. Such a deadly combination he always told her. Derrick was incarcerated for aggravated assault on Tamia's ex boyfriend. He used to stalk him and Tamia out of jealousy.

One day he took a swing at Derrick and shortly afterwards he was laying in the hospital in a coma. Derrick was training to be a boxer before he went to jail little did her ex know. Derrick was charged with attempted murder originally then it was reduced to aggravated assault.

"Hey Tamia why do you look like a deer caught in headlights you not happy to see your future husband?" He asked.

"That's your man Tamia he is fine?" Keisha asked.

"Yeah girl he is fine." Amber added.

"Thank you ladies." He responded with a blush.

"Come give daddy a hug Mi Mi." He said as he spread his arms wide open.

"You are not my daddy is your name on my birth certificate?" Tamia snapped at Derrick.

She always hated when men called themselves her daddy.

"No but your name is mud if I find out you been giving my loving away." He responded.

Sanaa was angry about that comment and it was written all over her face.

"Look we need to talk about a few things I'd rather not discuss them with you here so give me a number where I can reach you so we can meet up later." Tamia responded.

Derrick did exactly what she asked then kissed her on the cheek before he left.

"Tamia we need to talk can you step in the office for a minute?" Sanaa asked.

"Okay let me put her under the dryer first." Tamia responded.

She already knew what Sanaa wanted to talk about. They gave Derrick a threesome for his birthday before and Sanaa didn't want her seeing him at all. Tamia had deep feelings for him but she found out he was cheating so she stopped contact all together. The girl he was cheating with had a nerve to show her face in court even though she knew Tamia was his girlfriend.

After Tamia put her client under the dryer she went to see what kind of lecture Sanaa was about to give her.

"What's up S?" Tamia asked.

"Bitch I know you ain't about to start fucking with that nigga again are you? I told you I get jealous when anybody comes around you Mia you better tell that nigga we together and we live together he ain't getting none of my pussy and I mean that shit so you better tell him" Sanaa snapped.

"Alright S I already was going to tell him that's why I said not here relax you got me I'm not going anywhere chill." Tamia reassured her.

"Okay I'll calm down but I don't want to lose you Mia my feelings are involved now so can you understand if I start tripping a little bit about things like this?" Sanaa said trying to justify her actions.

"Yeah I can understand that's why I'm being patient with you because I know you get emotional when it comes to me." Tamia said as she kissed Sanaa on her cheek and went back to work.

"So who was that Tamia that nigga was fine is that your man because if it's not you need to hook a sister up." Keisha asked excitedly.

"No that is not her man that's her ex and he ain't all that." Sanaa responded as she rolled her eyes.

Sanaa did not want that conversation to take place.

"She must be jealous." Amber said playfully.

"Yeah must be." Keisha agreed with a smirk on her face.

Sanaa didn't find anything funny.

"Ain't nobody jealous, and you two bitches need to shut up and do some hair." Sanaa responded.

That's all she could think of to say at that moment. But deep down inside she was in love with Tamia and didn't care who knew. But she didn't want Tamia going through the motions of dealing with people not agreeing with two females being together. Sanaa on the other hand didn't care personally about what other people had to say. She was in love and that's all that mattered to her. She wanted to tell Keisha and Amber that but thought they might quit because of it they were good stylist and she didn't want to lose them.

"Anyway I didn't hear Tamia say anything so what's up Tamia" Keisha responded not letting the conversation go.

"I rather not discuss it" Tamia responded.

She knew the conversation was getting to Sanaa by the way she reacted. Later that night Tamia called Derrick and they made arrangements to meet at Boots and Bonnets for a drink after the shop closed. No way was Sanaa going to let Tamia go alone just in case she was sucked back into his charm and that was something she wasn't about to let happen.

"Are you ready Tamia?" Sanaa asked.

"Yeah I'm ready but first you have to promise me you will not cause a scene in this bar." Tamia said knowing her girlfriend very well.

"Okay I promise." Sanaa answered.

"Okay well lets go I want to get this over with quick so I can go to bed I'm tired." Tamia said.

"Yeah me too come on." Sanaa agreed.

When they got to the bar Derrick was already waiting.

"Sanaa sit over here at this table let me talk to him alone first." Tamia suggested.

"Well why I can't hear the conversation?" Sanaa asked.

"Because breaking something like this to him will be better if I did it alone maybe he'll take it better." Tamia responded.

"But what if he don't if he going to snap he going to snap regardless" Sanaa reasoned.

"All right well come on." Tamia responded.

She knew if she kept insisting it would cause an argument between her and Sanaa because of her insecurity.

"Hello Derrick" Tamia spoke as she sat down next to him.

"Tamia you are looking lovely as ever and how are you Sanaa?" Derrick greeted the ladies.

"I'm fine, Tamia tell him skip the small talk." Sanaa said.

"Tell me what Tamia?" Derrick asked.

"Sanaa and I are a couple now so if you're coming back to start over with me it's not going to happen because we live together and she's very over protective and jealous. I couldn't tell you this in the shop because our stylists don't know we're bisexual." Tamia responded.

"Sounds like you two are lesbians to me." Derrick responded sarcastically.

"So what if we are? You wasn't saying that when we gave you that threesome you just mad you can't get no more pussy from Tamia because it's mine." Sanaa snapped.

"Sanaa." Tamia said through clinched teeth.

"What did we just talk about before we came here and you're still making a scene anyway, calm down this is why I told you to sit over there I knew this was going to happen." Tamia continued.

"I'm sorry but he needs to watch his mouth" Sanaa continued to snap.

"Bitch, don't tell me what I need to do, fucking dike." Derrick angrily snapped back.

"Oh Derrick you need to watch that shit and as a matter of fact on that note we're calling it a night don't use that number I called you from and we can't be friends either because if you think that way about her I know you think that way about me, so it was nice seeing you again and tell that bitch you was cheating on me with I said hello goodbye Derrick." Tamia responded then took Sanaa by her hand and left the bar.

Once they got back in the Escalade Tamia started to snap.

"What the fuck I tell you about causing scenes I had that under control I didn't need you to step in Sanaa." Tamia snapped as she switched gears from park to drive.

"I'm sorry Tamia I'll make it up to you." Sanaa said as she rubbed her hand up Tamia's thigh.

"You always trying to butter me up when you know you wrong and I'm mad at you." Tamia responded.

Sanaa then moved in for the kill as she put her hand up her shirt. This made Tamia swerve a little bit before she gained control of the wheel. What she was just upset about was completely forgotten. She knew just what to do to make Tamia's eyes roll in the back of her head especially when she was mad. That was her way of getting off the hook with Tamia and it worked each and every time. Tamia stepped on the gas so they could get there faster because Sanaa had her hot and bothered.

"I never thought a female would have this affect on me she knows just how to touch me where and when as if she's reading my mind." Tamia thought to herself.

"Everyday I'm hustling, everyday I'm hustling." interrupted by an alert.

"Hit me up in the morning I'm busy." Tamia answered.

"Okay Spazz don't get mad if I hit you up at the crack of dawn tomorrow all right." Juice responded.

"Yeah all right nigga just hit me up tomorrow." Tamia responded.

She never knew she supplied Hutch and his rival Juice because if she did she would have cut Juice off. Hutch was a loyal customer and her sweetheart. She had an attraction to Hutch but never let on because she didn't mix business with pleasure Sanaa was an exception after all they were friends first.

"Who was that Tamia?" Sanaa asked soft and sweet because she knew the way she had Tamia feeling she could ask anything and get the answer.

"Oh that was a customer no threat to my baby though." Tamia said as she was enjoying the feeling.

"I love when you touch me like that I got a surprise for you when we get in the house." Tamia continued. "

What is it?" Sanaa asked anxiously.

"Wait until we get inside my goodness." Tamia said playfully rolling her eyes.

Sanaa couldn't help but to burst into laughter. When they got home Tamia told Sanaa to close her eyes and wait in the kitchen so she wouldn't see where her hiding spot was for the next time she decided to buy Sanaa a present.

"All right open them." Tamia said when she went back into the kitchen.

"Wow it's so beautiful thank you so much." Sanaa said as she admired the Tennis bracelet she pulled out of the box.

She showed Tamia just how much she liked the bracelet. That was a night neither one of them would ever forget their bond got even stronger. Tamia was always doing romantic things for Sanaa especially after she expressed how she felt about her. The three words I love you meant so much to Tamia that it made her hold nothing back as far as romance after all, let her tell it she wrote the book on it.

The next morning Juice kept his promise he alerted Tamia at the crack of dawn.

"Everyday I'm hustling, everyday I'm hustling." came through the speakers.

"Yizzo" Tamia answered her chirp.

"Can I see you now are you still busy?" Juice asked.

"Yeah you can see me give me an hour I'll come to you." Tamia responded.

She was feeling like a new woman after the night she just had.

"I get money, money I got, I get, I get money." another alert came through her phone.

"What's up Hutch long time no hear what's good?" Tamia answered.

"Ain't shit Spazz I need the usual I got shot baby girl I had to recover now I got to get back at it." Hutch responded.

"Oh yeah, Delaware off the hook like Chester huh all this shooting got to stop you good though? Why didn't you hit me up I would've came up there to see you, you know you my little sweetheart." Tamia responded.

Sanaa shot Tamia a look that could kill.

"I'm playing girl relax." Tamia said.

Sanaa rolled her eyes and layed back down.

"Who are you calling little? And they had to take one of my lungs

out. I got shot in the neck I'm good though how long you talking?"
Hutch asked.

"Like an hour and a half." Tamia responded.

"All right bet." Hutch answered.

"I'll be back babe I got to go get this money I love you." Tamia said
before she kissed Sanaa's cheek.

When Sanaa sat up she had a tear running down her face.

"What's wrong S?" Tamia asked.

"You just said what I was waiting for you to say for a long time now
I love you too Tamia. I can tell by your actions but I never heard you say
it so when are you going to stop hustling all together?" Sanaa asked.

"I mean we bring in enough money at the shop and I know you got a
nice stash from both the weed and the dope so don't you think it's about
time you gave it up. I don't want anything to happen to you Tamia what
am I going to do if you go to jail?" Sanaa asked.

"I will when I sell the rest of the weed I have right now I won't re- up
let me go and come back before you make me start tearing up." Tamia
said trying to hold back the tear that was about to fall.

"All right Tamia be careful baby." Sanaa said.

"I will go back to sleep." Tamia responded.

"Damn, why did she have to get all sentimental on me early in the
morning?" Tamia thought to herself.

Juice was outside on the phone when she pulled up.

"Yeah I'm ready to trunk this nigga just let me get a little more paper
first so I can step right in and take over after I lullaby his ass. I'm ready
to put an end to this cat and mouse game I heard he was back home but
nobody seen him on the stroll when you see that nigga setting up shop
holla." Juice said before hanging up the phone.

Over hearing the conversation Tamia couldn't make out who he was
talking to or about.

"All right nigga come on I got shit to do let's make this quick." Tamia
said getting agitated.

"My bad Spazz a nigga got drama, here go your change mami, you
can count it, it's all there." Juice responded.

"You know I will I don't trust a single soul." Tamia answered back.

"I'll holla though I got another crack of dawn nigga to go holla at. Oh and Juice you need to handle your business out here, not saying you're not, but you need to get that gwap up and make a big purchase that'll last you a long time because you're going to have to look for a new connect because my baby wants me to stop hustling. Once I'm done what I got I'm done." Tamia explained.

"What?" You can't quit on me now, I just started eating a little bit I need some time how long you talking before you quit ma?" Juice asked disappointedly.

"I don't know six months tops. I just hope y'all niggas hurry up I don't want it to take that long I'm trying to stop ASAP." Tamia responded as she turned to leave.

"I'm making my baby worry too much about me being in the streets." Tamia continued.

"I can understand that because if you were my girl I wouldn't want you out here either but damn you just dropped a bomb on a nigga." Juice responded.

"Thanks for understanding I just thought I'd give you a heads up I'm out play pimping." Tamia said with a smirk on her face.

"Now why I got to be play pimping, why not just pimping?" Juice said half offended.

"Jokes just jokes I'll holla" Tamia said as she drove off.

On her way to meet Hutch, Sanaa alerted her.

"What's up babe?" Tamia answered.

"Just checking on you to make sure you were okay and to ask you a question." Sanaa responded.

"Go head baby ask me anything." Tamia said with a smile on her face.

"Can we spend the rest of the day together without you answering any more drug related calls, I want us to do what we haven't done in a very long time Mia I want us to have fun let's go to the movies or Dave & Buster's and relive our childhood a little bit, or go to Warm Daddy's or Temptations and get our grown woman on, please Mia just me and you today no phone no shop no nothing just us." Sanaa asked in a child-like voice.

Tamia couldn't help but to give in.

"Anything for my baby no phone just me and you and I told one of my customers that I was giving the game up in a few more months and I'm on my way to tell the other one I'm giving it all up to make you happy Sanaa. I don't want you visiting me behind bars or coming to my funeral." Tamia said letting what she said earlier sink in.

Excited Sanaa made a squealing noise that took Tamia by Surprise she swerved and didn't see the police car until the officer turned his lights on.

"Oh shit S you made me swerve with that noise in front of a cop and he pulling me over stay by the phone in case I need bail money my car legit but in case he smells the weed ok baby?" Tamia said nervously trying to remain calm.

"Of course just relax and everything will be cool boo." Sanaa answered.

"All right license and registration please." The officer asked wasting no time. Tamia handed the officer what he asked for.

"Okay ma'am if everything is ok I'll let you go with a warning." The officer said before he walked away.

When the cop started to walk back to his car Tamia started to pray that he didn't smell the aroma of marijuana coming from her car. The smell was so strong it was over riding the air freshener she had hanging from the rearview. The officer finally came back after fifteen minutes.

"Okay you're free to go, what caused you to swerve to begin with?" The officer asked.

"My girlfriend squealed through the phone and it startled me that's it." She answered upset he wanted to hold a conversation.

"Okay ma'am careful next time you can cause an accident like that." He responded.

"I will Mr. Officer." she responded as she pulled off before he even took a second step.

"That was a close call." She thought to herself as she alerted Sanaa.

"What's up what happened?" Sanaa asked.

"He let me go with a warning stop talking to me when you know I'm dirty that was a close call you was about to be sending me commissary." Tamia snapped.

"But I'm not and you're coming home so go handle your business and hurry up so we can spend the day together." Sanaa said as she laughed at Tamia's comment.

"All right girl." She responded as she headed to Wilmington to meet Hutch.

When she got there he looked like he lost a lot of weight and the scar on his neck was ugly as ever.

"Hutch what the fuck happened?" Tamia asked not used to seeing her sweetheart like that.

"I'm beefing with some nigga over what he likes to think is his project, that nigga did ten years where was he at when me and Starsky got this shit popping like it's popping now fuck that nigga he ain't punking me when I see him he's dead and that's real rap. I'm salty he got away when we had that motherfucker he ended up killing my cousin Eric, you know he was the one that killed Starsky so you know he's a dead man walking." Hutch responded angrily losing his breathe in the process.

"Damn Hutch you ain't beefing you at war my nigga but listen I'm out the game in like six months so I'm giving you a heads up so you can look for another connect. I'm done I'm retiring while I still can." Tamia explained.

"I hear you Spazz maybe one day I can retire but for now I need revenge on that nigga it's personal it ain't about the project he killed my right hand man and my cousin I'm lost without Starsky, he took half my heart away from me, I got ice running through my veins now." Hutch said with a look of rage in his eyes.

"I can't begin to feel your pain about your cousin but your right hand man I can relate to that one but the pain still doesn't go away after you get revenge. I can tell you first hand but if that's what you seek then that's what you seek. But I will be the one to tell you to be careful out here I don't want to see you behind bars for life behind some bullshit that's food for thought play boy I'm out you be safe." Tamia said after they made the exchange.

"All right Spazz I hope you enjoy your retirement in six months ma you deserve it with your sexy self." Hutch responded.

That comment made Tamia blush as she pulled off.

"Wow he is fine but Sanaa would have a fit if I started dealing with him and besides he's in too much drama. I had enough of that shit anyway let me go start the day off with my girl right we going to breakfast." Tamia thought to herself as she searched through her IPOD for one song in particular.

Since she brought an IPOD she didn't carry cd's around anymore her IPOD was her best friend.

"Ahh there it is." She said to herself aloud when she found the song.

"The only thing that keeps me up when I'm feeling down I don't know about you but I got to keep mines around I done looked I done searched but it's hard to find another Shorty like mine baby that's why." She sang along with Bow Wow and Chris Brown as she headed down Interstate 495 on her way back to Chester.

Once she got back to the apartment Sanaa greeted her with a hug and a long kiss.

"What's that for?" Tamia asked.

"Because you made it home to me that's why." Sanaa responded.

Tamia took that moment to show Sanaa exactly how much she loved her, afterwards they fell asleep.

When Tamia woke up she just stared at Sanaa sleeping for ten minutes before Sanaa opened her eyes.

"What's wrong Mia?" Sanaa asked.

"I was just watching you sleep you ready to go eat I did want to take you to breakfast but since I had you for breakfast we can have lunch then go to Dave & Buster's come on get dressed." Tamia responded.

"Okay Mia we going to have some fun today." Sanaa said as she made her way to the shower. Tamia's phone rang.

"Hello" Tamia answered.

"Spazz hi how are you?" Hector asked.

"Maintaining how are things with you?" Tamia responded.

"I miss seeing your pretty face I would like to talk to you though, when can we get together to discuss a few things." Hector asked.

"Well today's no good I have a date with my girlfriend so maybe tomorrow I'll call you and let you know when, is everything okay?" Tamia asked.

"I'll talk to you when I see you tomorrow this isn't a phone conversation." Hector said.

Hector never liked discussing anything over the phone.

"Okay I'll see you tomorrow." Tamia ended the conversation.

After she hung up she heard the shower cut off.

"Damn I wanted to join her in the shower I guess I have to shower alone." Tamia thought to herself.

CHAPTER EIGHT:

ON TOP

"Damn Flex I never thought we would be where we are right now man fifty bricks I can't believe it." Fats said.

"I can't believe Spazz actually wanted to give this shit up and miss all this money to live a normal life I can't see it." Flex responded shaking his head.

"Yeah I know a hair shop don't make you feel like you on top of the world like this dope money do." Fats responded.

"I hear you partner I hear you I ain't know the dude Carlos was related to Spazz's connect I hope Hector don't find out we killed him so we can take his territory over." Flex added.

"As long as you stop talking about it neither Spazz nor Hector will find out and stop saying Spazz connect he's our Connect now just like these blocks here in Philly we controlling this is our shit now." Fats said in an angry tone.

It never sat right with him that he was working for a female.

"All right but if she finds out Cash was an inside job and Carlos, without permission she can end our career on these streets." Flex said bringing the obvious to his attention.

Flex still had love for Tamia deep down inside he really didn't want to cross her but his greed had too much influence over him. It was too late for him to turn back now he already bit the hand that fed him. He was knee deep into this shit Fats called an on top of the world feeling. He wanted to tell Tamia everything real bad but didn't know how or when in the back of his mind he knew Fats would do the same shiesty thing to him one day if he blinked his eyes for too long.

Fats had been acting more like Flex's power struck boss than his partner he just wanted things back the way they were before. Fats never thought Flex was built for this game. He only made him partner because he needed him to get close to Tamia knowing she would be vulnerable after they took out her right hand man. He planned on killing as soon as they reached one hundred kilos of cocaine. His greed left him with no regard for human life let alone their feelings.

"Spazz ain't ending nobody's career every time she had somebody rocked, one of us did it, I never saw her pull no trigger." Fats said getting even more upset.

"Just because you never saw her don't mean she never did you forgot one of the main rules never under estimate anyone." Flex reminded him.

"So what like I said she soft I can tell by the way she acted after we sung Cash a lullaby then basically gave us the whole business I knew she was going to fall for that let us take over the blocks shit and you be our connect you dig but I never thought she would give up the connect that was a plus." Fats said as he chuckled like an evil genius.

"Yeah it was but I don't feel right about this she was good to us the whole time we was working for her I think we went about this wrong." Flex tried to reason.

"Yeah well it's a dog eat dog world either you built or you not." Fats said nonchalantly.

"All right Fats let's just bag this work up so we can get this paper okay." Flex suggested getting irritated.

They were so busy arguing that they never heard the door unlock or open and close when they were in the kitchen of Tamia's first stash house. They never knew she was coming nor did they know she was going to have Hector with her. Tamia and Hector were meeting there to talk when they over heard the conversation after they finished eaves dropping they crept back out after one of them turned on the radio.

"Follow me to the Capitol Grill Hec we can talk there." Tamia said in an angry tone.

Hector nodded agreeing. When they made it to the restaurant they began their conversation after they were seated.

"I can't believe what the fuck I just heard, in the back of my mind I knew their story didn't add up about what happened to Cash. But Carlos too I never would have seen that one coming it's official, they are done on the streets of Philly. I knew it would be a matter of time before the truth finally came out. I was right about Flex he does have a good heart but is easily influenced, and Fats I was always suspicious when he started acting like he was on his best behavior but I never could figure out exactly who killed Cash until now." Tamia began.

"Yeah that's what I wanted to meet with you about. When you told me they were to take over. I thought you were slipping because I knew they killed Cash. I didn't say anything because I wanted to see how you handled the situation. But when you said you were out I thought you were giving up because of Cash's death. But keeping it inside was eating me up so that's why I called you I also knew they were using the house without your permission. See Guns is my family not blood but it couldn't make us any closer. I sent him to work for you because I wanted to make sure you were protected at all times. I fell in love with you the first day we met Spazz, out of respect for Derrick I didn't say anything. Can I call you Tamia I hate having to call such a beautiful woman such an ugly name but before you answer let me finish, Carlos isn't dead we staged the funeral to make them think that he was. He's almost fully recovered but however if you want this to happen Carlos is going to kill the both of them and from my understanding their workers aren't very happy with their pay so we can use that to plan our attack, oh and by the way you wanting to meet at the house was perfect I knew they'd be there because they just scored from me, so what's your outlook on the situation?" Hector asked as he finished what he had to say.

"So when were you going to tell me you were spying on me and you were in love with me?" Tamia asked. "And I'll have to think about letting you call me Tamia for now don't give them any more bricks let them niggas sweat from here on out don't answer their calls let them assume that your locked up and when they blow your horn up let me know how many times they call. We are going to let them dumb niggas self destruct first then we going to hit them in the mean time tell Guns I want to see him tell him to meet me at the Ruth Chris down the street at eight thirty tonight." Tamia said angrily.

"Look, don't be mad at me I was only trying to make sure my queen was safe I'll let Guns know what's up and I'll be in touch." Hector responded feeling like a lot of weight was lifted off his shoulders.

"Oh by the way Carlos said to tell you hi." Hector added.

"Tell him I said hi." Tamia responded with a confused look on her face.

Hector excused himself then left while Tamia waited for her food.

"What the fuck just when I thought I was done with this shit, well at least I have closure I know for sure it was them niggas but Hector took me by surprise with his shit. So he knew all along this shit was going down, now I know how he knew about Cash so quick that sneaky motherfucker." She thought to herself as the waiter brought her food to the table.

"I have to pull this off without Sanaa knowing anything she'll kill me if she finds out I have to go back to this life for even a second." She continued thinking as the waiter walked away.

As she bit into one of the delicious crab cakes she ordered she came up with the ultimate plan and needed Guns to play his part.

"So these dudes think I'm soft huh, these dudes don't think I can end their career on the streets huh, oh we'll see about that we going to see what's what I made them niggas I definitely will break their asses." She thought as she enjoyed her crab cakes.

When she finished her meal she went to spend some time with Sanaa before her meeting with Guns.Since they took a small vacation from the shop to spend some quality time together.

Later on that night Tamia's personality split as she turned on to Broad Street Tamia left and Spazz took over. To her surprise she immediately found a parking spot.

"I must be V.I.P tonight." Tamia thought to herself.

When she got inside the hostess greeted her very politely.

"How many ma'am?" She asked.

"May I have a table for two please my party should be arriving in about ten minutes." Tamia responded.

"In about ten seconds you mean, I'm already here baby girl I would never keep your sexiness waiting." Guns interrupted as he entered.

"Hello handsome how are you?" Tamia responded.

"Well you two come with me while I seat you would you like a table or booth?" The hostess asked.

"Booth." They said in unison.

"Okay your waitress will be with you shortly." The hostess said as she turned to walk away.

"Thank you." Tamia responded.

"So you wanted to see me Tamia I'm sorry Spazz I never would've guessed your name was Tamia you look like your name should be something exotic." Guns began the conversation.

"Don't you ever say my government name out loud again and why didn't you tell me Hector was your peoples?" Tamia asked angrily.

"I couldn't, he told me not to say anything." Guns said getting defensive.

"Anyway I need to know some details about a few things and if you don't already know then I need you to get the details you dig." Tamia got right to the point.

"You need details on what?" Guns asked.

"Like how often these fools re-up, where's their stash spot, where do they lay their necks, how many workers are unhappy, who their girlfriends are and where they live, where they hang out I want to know everything I have a plan but I need those details to piece it all together." Tamia said like she was the boss of an Italian mob crime family.

"Well I can tell you where the stash house is, Hector knows how often they re-up and everyone is unhappy, I know some places they hang out at and the rest I need to find out." Guns replied.

"All right then tell Hector when they call remember not to answer, we going to rob these niggas first we taking everything money, dope, and any guns they got we stripping them niggaz naked like they was before I put them on. They done got way too big for their britches mommy got to spank them and make them remember I'm a boss before we sing them a lullaby. You know what I'm talking about?" Tamia said with a deranged look in her eyes and a smirk.

"Yeah, I know exactly what you talking about." Guns answered liking the idea.

"So, those niggas are up to like fifty bricks now huh?" Tamia asked.

"I'll let them knock some of that off first before I hit them make sure you play your position Guns I need every detail then get back to me ASAP." Tamia said.

"No problem, I fucks with you real hard Spazz. I never met a female like you you're a rare breed and I respect that to the fullest." Guns responded with a smile.

"Thank you I didn't know you were so charming." Tamia responded.

"That's because you were all business we never got to have a one on one like this. But I got to fall back though because I'm so attracted to you, and so is my man Hector, Carlos and some of your old workers you don't know what affect you have on men. But we're going to eat and I'll get on that info for you ASAP." Guns responded like she just took his last breath away from him.

"I never picked up on any of that but we can stop discussing it since this is uncomfortable for the both of us make sure you tell Hector even though I know you won't forget and as soon as them niggas get down to twenty five to thirty bricks let me know that's when we attack." Tamia responded.

When the waitress finally came with their order they ate in silence. When Tamia got home Sanaa was fast asleep. A week went by and like Tamia promised she hit Fats and Flex's stash house and took everything they had in there. They weren't smart enough to keep things separate they had all of their money, cocaine, and guns in the same stash house. When Tamia took what she got to her spot she counted up everything.

She couldn't believe they actually stacked up two point five million, ten bricks, and three hundred thousand dollars worth of bagged up cocaine and ten guns.

"Like my dude Kane said in Menace to Society better me than the police." She thought to herself as she laughed wishing she could see the look on their faces when they found out they got robbed. She waited a week before she called Guns.

"Hello." Guns answered.

"What's up my dude? It's done tell your peoples to expect a phone call if he hasn't gotten any already and tell him I want him to answer the phone and tell them niggas I said they are finished on the streets they gets no more work." Tamia started the conversation.

"Okay Spazz I'm on it." Guns responded.

"Oh and I need to see you in two days so meet me at Fat Tuesday's on South Street at eight o'clock." Tamia added.

"No problem." Guns said before hanging up.

"I wonder how they're going to react to that I'm a boss they must have forgot. This is war now but I have to make it interesting." Tamia thought to herself as her phone rang.

"Hello." She answered.

"Mia where are you? I miss you and I have this strange feeling that you're in the streets again because of the way you've been acting please tell me you're not hustling." Sanaa said in an angry tone.

"No I'm not I got to handle something though everything will be back to normal in a minute sweetie I promise matter of fact I'm on my way home soon." Tamia responded.

"Okay I'm waiting." Sanaa responded.

"Damn her woman's intuition must have kicked in." Tamia thought to herself.

When Tamia walked in the door Sanaa was sitting in a chair with her arms folded staring directly at her, she needed answers to the funny behavior. When Tamia saw the look she already knew what she was in store for and she was prepared.

"Hello sweetie I got something for you." Tamia said quickly to take Sanaa's mind off of the situation. Sanaa smiled instantly.

"So Mia what do you have for me is this what you were up to lately." Sanaa questioned.

She reached into the duffel bag and handed her a few stacks of hundreds equaling a hundred thousand dollars.

"I want you to go shopping for some furniture for our new house we're going to start looking real soon." Tamia said.

Sanaa had a big smile on her face after hearing the news.

"Can you give me a massage Sanaa my back is killing me." Tamia complained.

"No problem boo lay down but you got to strip first." Sanaa said smiling.

"Oh strip first huh you nasty." Tamia said with a smirk on her face.

"I'm nasty but you love it though." Sanaa said smiling.

"Your right I do but do I get the works or do I just get a full body massage." Tamia asked.

"Girl with that money you just gave me on top of the news you get the works and dinner cooked for you tomorrow night." Sanaa responded.

"You sounding like a gold digger right now, you don't just want me for my money do you?" Tamia asked with a sly look on her face.

"How can you say something like that?" You know I'm in love with you for you I don't want your money you can have it back." Sanaa said angrily as she folded her arms.

"Hold on Sanaa I was only playing if I thought you were with me for my money I wouldn't be with you. Now relax I know you love me you been holding me down for a while now I know what it is with you." Tamia reassured her.

"Well stop playing like that you know I'm sensitive." Sanaa responded.

"Yeah I know but sometimes I want to have fun with my girl I can't have fun with you?" Tamia asked.

"Well since you put it like that yeah you can have fun with me." Sanaa replied continuing the massage.

"I love you Sanaa." Tamia said as she was enjoying her massage.

"I love you too Mia." Sanaa responded.

A few days later Tamia met Guns on South Street to her surprise he was already there waiting.

"Hello Guns you're early." Tamia greeted.

"Yeah Spazz, I couldn't wait to see you." He responded with a smile.

"Wow I'm flattered what you got for me?" Tamia responded getting to the point.

"They almost went insane when they found out they got robbed, they looked like two sick puppies." Guns laughed.

"But that's not the half of it they called Hector and tried to explain the situation and actually had the nerve to ask for fifty birds on consignment." Guns continued.

"What did Hector say?" Tamia asked trying to hold in her laughter.

"He said hell no, first of all I don't trust you enough to front you fifty birds. Spazz is the only one I'd do that favor for. Since we're on the subject we know you two were the ones that killed Cash and Carlos. I know you guys didn't think you were going to get away with that are you serious? I have a message from Spazz also, you're finished on the streets of Philadelphia and your days are numbered you dumb motherfucker. Never bite the hand that feeds you. It can come back to haunt you but too bad you won't learn from your mistakes. Then he banged that was some gangster shit if you ask me I wish I could've seen the look on dude face when he pulled his ear away from the phone." Guns finished his news.

"I love Hector for that one I wish I was there to see the look on their faces too, is Carlos still up for this or do he still need time to heal?" Tamia asked.

"He's good he's ready." Guns responded.

"Okay tell him tomorrow night." Tamia responded.

"All right I'll tell him this 190 Octane got me fucked up Fat Tuesday's knows how to make a drink I'm done up." Guns responded.

"How many did you have?" Tamia inquired.

"I had two I only should've got one I'm going straight home." Guns said.

"All right you be safe don't get into any accidents or anything, oh wait I almost forgot I got a little gift for you." Tamia said as she handed him a bag.

"What's this?" Guns asked.

"It's three hundred thousand worth of bagged up work you take half of that and split it with the workers them sorry ass dudes had working for them." Tamia whispered in his ear.

"Damn what you Robin Hood Princess of thieves?" Guns joked.

"Yeah nigga now don't kick a gift horse in the mouth." She responded as she left Fat Tuesday's.

Meanwhile, "What the fuck are we going to do now Fats? I told your dumb ass this was going to happen you didn't want to listen. We ain't got shit now we went from having fifty bricks to having nothing at all not a gun, not a ounce, and I got about five hundred in my pocket to my name." Flex snapped.

"I don't know what we're going to do. I got like eight hundred to mine. And who the fuck Spazz think she is talking about we finished on the streets of Philly. Shit this is our city she ain't even from here." Fats snapped also.

"I don't know about you but I'm on a train to my peoples spot down Florida to lay low for awhile I can get back on my feet down there then come back to Philly you can come if you want but I'm out my cousin should be able to hook me up with a connect." Fats responded.

"I'm with you I don't have a choice." Flex responded.

"Spazz don't know who she fucking with I'm going to come up on my own then come back to rock that bitch that's my word." Fats spoke as he thought about the conversation he had with Hector.

"When are we leaving?" Flex asked.

"Tomorrow or the day after but I want to know where Guns, Kurt, and Hammer got work from they was posted on the block earlier." Fats answered as he wondered.

"Oh yeah, I wonder if they robbed us." Flex responded.

"I don't know but I'll figure this shit out when we get to Florida I'll meet you at 30th Street station at eight o'clock the day after tomorrow." Fats responded.

He had no intentions on taking Flex to Florida with him. He also lied about how much money he had he actually had about thirty five hundred and planned on setting up shop down in Florida never returning to Philly. There was no way Fats was going to be killed by a female he couldn't see it. Especially while he was unarmed he was a sitting duck. He decided to drive down instead of catching the train. He left that same night traveling down interstate I95 all the way to his cousin's house only stopping for gas.

Flex went to the train station at eight o'clock two days later like Fats asked him to do. After waiting for two hours he realized Fats wasn't going to show up. He tried calling but his phone went to voicemail every time. As soon as he turned to leave he was approach by Guns, Hammer, and Kurt.

"So Flex, where do you think you're going?" Hammer asked.

"I guess y'all here for Spazz huh?" Flex asked.

"Nah nigga she said dead or alive it's more alive so you coming with us you bitch ass nigga." Kurt said before he punched him in his face and drew blood from his nose.

Hammer followed up with a punch and Guns couldn't resist getting in a few hits. They threw him in the car and sped off. When they pulled up to the old stash house Guns made him open the door.

"Open this motherfucking door I know you got the key." Guns demanded.

Flex was moving too slow so Guns reached in his pocket and took it out himself. Once they got inside they tied Flex to the chair.

"Where is your ungrateful partner at huh it's more money for the both of y'all and I want my change." Kurt said before he smacked him with the butt of the gun.

"Get Spazz on the phone." Hammer said.

"I'm already on it." Guns replied.

"Oh you ain't going to talk." Kurt asked before he hit him again.

"Yo we got one of these dudes at the spot and he still got air you on your way." Guns asked.

"Yeah" Tamia said on the other end.

"We are going to beat the shit out of you until you talk now where he at?" Kurt said as he continued to beat him until he finally talked.

"He went to Florida to his cousin house I was supposed to go with him but he left me. That's why I was at the train station." Flex pleaded.

"So why are you protecting this nigga after he hung you out to dry?" Guns asked.

"I'm not protecting him he never told me where his cousin lives all I know is he went to Florida." Flex continued to plead.

"All right that's enough we'll let Spazz deal with this nut ass nigga when she gets here." Guns order.

As soon as the words left his mouth Flex looked like he saw a ghost when he saw Carlos walk through the door.

"I thought you were dead you had a fucking funeral and everything" Flex said amazed.

"Surprised to see me huh?" Carlos said with a smirk on his face being sarcastic.

"Did you and Fats really think you were going to get away with this shit lucky for me I always come to the block with my vest on but why Cash after Spazz treated you ungrateful motherfuckers like family and y'all cross her like this?" Carlos asked.

"Yeah this ungrateful cocksucker crossed me backstabbing bastard." Tamia said as she joined the party.

"Spazz so glad you could join us any last words before I rock this son of a bitch?" Carlos asked.

"Yeah why the fuck you kill Cash and where the hell is that nigga Fats I want that nigga head." Tamia said as she shot him in his knee.

"He's in Florida that's all I know he in Florida." Flex said as he burst in to tears.

"Man up nigga, stop crying like a little bitch this is a grown man game if you weren't built you shouldn't have played. Spazz is a woman and play this shit just like a man would, you are a fucking pussy in my eyes, a pussy on his ninth life goodbye motherfucker." Carlos said as he put the gun to his head and squeezed. "Now that's how you rock a nigga look him in his eyes and squeeze with no hesitation." Guns said cheering Carlos on.

"Enough, this is not a happy moment you do what you have to do when you have to do it you don't celebrate about it." Tamia angrily responded.

" Yo clean this shit up and dump this nigga body somewhere." Carlos added.

"Oh and here's a brick for each of you good work for bringing this nigga to me alive now if you find Fats bitch ass I got another brick for you." Tamia said.

"I can use that." Guns responded.

"Well then find that nigga and bring him back to Philly alive dead you only get half a brick." Tamia snapped then went back home to Sanaa.

Carlos went back to Jersey and the boys did what they were told they cleaned up and got rid of the body.

CHAPTER NINE:

THE FIGHT FOR DELAWARE

Hutch was back in business he was only working with ten pounds again but the way he had shit popping he'd flip that in to twenty pounds in no time. He was feeling insecure about the scar on his neck but the girls always loved Hutch. Even though they let him know he was still handsome with the scar, he didn't like it and planned on getting a tattoo to cover it.

The next day he did just that getting Souljah tatted over the scar. He had a good heart but at the same time took no crap from anybody. He had a look out at every entrance to the project. They weren't look outs for the cops they were look outs for Juice. Hutch set aside twenty five thousand dollars that he refused to touch for whom ever knows Juice's whereabouts or sees him creeping through the project. He vowed to revenge his cousin and best friend's deaths.

"Yo Sherelle come here with your sexy self girl." Hutch spoke.

"Hey Hutch I like the tatt on your neck when did you get it?" Sherelle asked.

"Today you can't tell how fresh it is?" Hutch responded with lust in his eyes. He hadn't had sex with Sherelle since Starsky was still alive and he missed being inside her womanhood. He remembered how warm and wet she felt as soon as he saw her.

"So what's up with you, are you done beefing with that old head?" She asked.

"Yeah I'm still beefing with that nigga why you asking matter of fact, fuck him when can I dig up in your insides again I miss that twat." He responded angry she brought the situation up.

"Come pass my house tonight when you get done out here, why don't you give me a bag of weed so I can get my mind right." Sherelle asked.

"Here girl and don't have no clothes on when I get there." Hutch responded as he handed her a bag.

He hadn't had sex since the day before he got shot and planned on making up for lost time when he got over there. When he finished talking to Sherelle he had twenty people waiting to be served. It seemed like the whole state of Delaware smoked weed and they all went to Hutch to buy it. Well that's how it seemed to him anyway.

"Glad to see you back Hutch." One of the guys said as he got served.

"Thanks man glad to be back." Hutch responded.

After a long day Hutch went home to count his money and he actually made four thousand that day. This made him feel like he was getting back on track he needed some sex to top it all off. He headed to Sherelle's house to get it. To his surprise she listened Sherelle was completely naked when he got there. She was smoking the marijuana he gave her earlier in the day.

"Let me hit that." Hutch said after he shut the door.

"Are you sure you can smoke with one lung?" Sherelle asked out of concern for her lover.

"Yeah I'm sure I do what I want." He responded.

After he took a few puffs he proceeded to kiss all over Sherelle until he made her hot and horny enough to attack him. After he slid his manhood inside of her warm insides she moaned immediately which turned Hutch on even more. He started hitting all the right spots making her yearn for more until they both climaxed and fell asleep. Hutch woke up around three thirty in the morning and left Sherelle's house. He had no intention of staying the night. He had to get back out there for the late night smokers, even potheads needed marijuana in the wee hours of the morning.

After Hutch got the early morning money he headed back to the house to take a nap. He was awakened by a phone call that someone had an M-16 for sale. Hutch wasted no time going to buy that weapon now that he was at war with Juice. Besides he had a fetish for guns he wanted anything anyone had to sell him.

After he brought it he went back to the strip to get some more money. Hutch kept getting this strange feeling in his gut he knew something was wrong. He ignored it but still stayed on his P's & Q's while he was out there making his money. By nightfall Hutch was tired and called it a night.

About six weeks later he got a phone call from Sherelle.

"Hello" Hutch answered.

"Hutch I'm pregnant I want this baby but I want the baby to have his or her father I don't want to wake up and find out someone killed you so tell me what you want me to do." Sherelle responded in tears.

"I want you to keep it of course, that's my child I mean, I wasn't ready for another child but since you're pregnant you're not killing my child I'm not having that." Hutch responded.

Sherelle remained silent not really knowing what else to say.

"Since you're pregnant I have to move you out of Delaware I don't want that nigga trying to kill you and our baby that would send me over the edge." Hutch added.

"Well where am I going to move to? I don't know any where else but Riverside and Southside." Sherelle asked still crying.

"You can go to Chester my peoples will make you feel at home Sherelle just trust me on this." Hutch responded.

"After he hung up he started making calls to his people in Chester, preparing to move his new baby momma out of Delaware. By the end of the month she was completely moved out of Riverside. It was just in time too because the day after she moved. One of the lookouts spotted Juice down the block and immediately called Hutch.

"What's up Baby Boy?" Hutch answered.

"Yo I seen this nigga down the street what you want me to do?" Baby Boy asked.

"Yo if you can wet that nigga up do it if not try to follow that cocksucker to where he going." Hutch ordered.

After Baby Boy hung up he crept down the block to where he seen Juice until he got close enough to open fire on him. Juice heard the shots and dove behind the nearest car after a bullet flew pass his head.

"Damn Hutch you sneaking up on a nigga huh, I heard your dumb ass was on frontline waiting on me, I had to get my paper right so I can take this project over after I kill your punk ass." Juice shouted after the bullets stopped.

"I ain't Hutch nigga but I'm riding for him." Baby Boy shouted back as he started firing again.

He shattered the car window Juice was behind. As the glass fell on him it cut his arms up.

"Damn this nigga got me bleeding and shit." Juice thought to himself as he started returning shots.

He hit a dog and the car in front of Baby Boy. Juice knew Baby Boy wouldn't pop his head up any time soon so he made his way to the next car. While Juice was making his move Baby Boy called another look out on the phone for some help. As soon as he hung up Juice was in position to hit Baby Boy as soon as he popped his head up. After Baby Boy heard silence he popped his head up to see if he saw Juice and was shot in the same arm he was holding his gun. The other lookout showed up while Juice was trying to close in on Baby boy. He started firing hitting Juice in the leg. But that didn't stop Juice he returned shots as he ran to his car. One of the bullets shot the second lookout right in the chest.

"Fuck, these niggas almost cornered me I wasn't prepared for this shit." Juice said aloud to no one in particular.

Juice finally made it to his car after bleeding along the way. The third lookout heard the shots and ran to the scene he made it in time to see Juice pulling away. He fired at the car hitting the back window but Juice kept driving. This nigga got this project on lock for real I never expected this from that nigga who would've thought." Juice said aloud to himself as he headed straight to his apartment complex.

The woman that lived above him was an RN. He was sleeping with her so he knew she could remove the bullet from his leg. He didn't want to draw attention by going to the hospital he already knew both the men he shot would end up there. He didn't want to be questioned by the police so she was convenient.

"What on earth happened to you?" The RN asked when he got there.

"I got shot ain't it obvious." he responded in a sarcastic tone.

"Well you didn't have to get smart I was asking how it happened." The RN responded getting offended.

"Can you remove this bullet for me or what ma? I'm bleeding to death over here." Juice said getting to the point.

"Yeah I can remove it and I know, you're bleeding all over my apartment." She said sarcastically.

She began operating on Juice lucky for him she had the equipment to do it. After about an hour and a half she got it out and bandaged him up. After she gave him some aspirin she sent him home to get some rest.

"What the fuck am I getting myself into dealing with this thug? First a bullet grazed him and now I'm removing a bullet out of his leg what next?" She asked herself as she cleaned the blood up Juice had dripped all over her apartment.

Juice was feeling so drained he went straight to sleep thinking he had to do something special for his personal nurse.

Meanwhile Baby Boy and the other lookout were mad they missed their chance at some real money. "Baby Boy, call Hutch and tell him that nigga got away." The third lookout said.

"You call him I'm shot motherfucker I'm supposed to be going to the hospital you bitch ass nigga I'm sitting here bleeding to death." Baby Boy snapped.

"Come on we'll call him on the way there." The lookout responded. He phoned Hutch as soon as he pulled off.

"Yo what up you got some good news for me or what?" Hutch answered the phone getting to the point.

"No we don't have no good news I'm on my way to take Baby Boy to the hospital this Shaheem, Son hit that nigga in the leg but caught one in the chest and that nigga still managed to get away Baby Boy got hit in the arm he should be all right though I'm mad as fuck I didn't get a chance to light that nigga up but a moving target is hard to hit you know what I mean?" Shaheem asked Hutch.

"Yeah I know what you mean unfortunately I'll holla at y'all later though." Hutch responded as he hung up the phone.

"This nigga is a pain in the ass I'm mad as fuck it's taking this long to kill this nigga now Baby Boy hit he could've gotten himself killed behind this bullshit." Hutch thought to himself.

He wanted this war to be over with fast especially with Sherelle being pregnant he didn't want his unborn child to grow up without a father because he knows what that feels like his father was killed when he was eight years old. Hutch left the apartment he got for Sherelle and went back to Delaware to see what was up with Baby Boy. He wanted to make sure his young buck was going to be okay. When he got to the hospital there were cops everywhere one detective was asking Baby Boy a thousand and one questions, about who shot him and was it any relation to the other shooting where Son was killed.

"No I don't know who shot me, him or what the fuck you talking about all I know is I heard shots and I ran I got hit in the arm now I'm here that's it you act like I'm a witness on the stand or something I'm a victim here getting treatment." Baby Boy snapped.

"Okay but if I find out you're telling a lie I will hold you responsible for the shooting and maybe even put you as the gunman, on trial for murder at eighteen you wouldn't see the light of day." The detective said as he walked out the door he eyed Hutch up and down recognizing him from Starsky's murder.

"Looks like your bad luck everyone you know ends up shot or killed

I wouldn't want to be friends with you." The detective said as he walked by Hutch.

Shaheem had to stop Hutch from attacking the detective.

"What the fuck you grab me for Sha that nigga need to watch his mouth with that bullshit my cousin and my right hand man is dead and he popping fly with that shit." Hutch snapped wanting to take his frustrations out on someone.

"I know Hutch that nigga's a nut ass dude son don't let him get to you that's what he wants to do get under your skin so you can react and as soon as you do he's putting the cuffs on you so chill." Shaheem said calming Hutch down.

"So what's up with Sherelle are y'all getting married after she have the baby or what my nigga?" Baby Boy asked trying to help Shaheem calm him down.

"I don't know man I got to get Juice disrespectful ass out the way first before I decide anything I don't want that nigga coming after my family you know I mean? I want my seed his or her mom to be safe my daughter and her mom moved to Baltimore already so I'm good there." Hutch responded letting his guard down a little bit.

He never expressed his feelings to anyone after Starsky died.

"We feeling your pain old head we miss Starsky too, I remember when I used to catch him as soon as he came outside, punch him in his stomach and run so he could chase me until he was out of breath when I was a young buck." Baby Boy reminisced aloud.

"Yeah, I remember that." Hutch said as he started laughing.

"Look we got to get out of here before that nut ass detective come back with more questions." Shaheem interrupted.

"Yeah I hear that I don't feel like talking to that prick or seeing his face." Hutch agreed.

"All right Hutch say no more we out of here let's go." Baby Boy said.

He was still drowsy from the medicine and couldn't really walk but he had to show his old head he was a soldier. They don't know how they slipped pass the guard but they were home free when they reached the stairway. They took Baby Boy to Hutch's house no one would look for him there. He could rest up without any bother from anyone. Hutch called a girl over to be Baby Boy's personal nurse while he got better. Hutch didn't want him back out until his arm was completely healed. As soon as he was he was back out there looking out for Juice.

If Juice did end up killing Hutch he would have to kill the new enemies that he just made as well.

"How can one man turn a whole city upside down like this not a single person was able to kill this nigga yet." Baby Boy thought to himself but still he was ready for war. Now that Baby Boy got shot, it started off being business to him now it was business and personal.

Juice was making a lot of enemies but he didn't care all he knew was he wanted Riverside back and the whole state of Delaware if it was possible. For a while Juice was too weak to go any farther than down stairs of his building. He had his clientele come to him which was a big mistake. As soon as he got better he started noticing a van parked outside with tinted windows in the same spot day after day. He decided to move to another complex because he was almost sure it was the FBI. He paid someone to rent him an apartment around the corner and move his stuff out of the old one. He had to stay in Claymont because he was wanted in Wilmington by Hutch and his soon to be army. He also wanted to stay close to his clientele so he wouldn't miss any money.

The Feds were at his apartment for a reason. They were aware of the killings. One of his neighbors called the police about his suspicious activity in their building. The Feds wanted Juice just as bad as Hutch did for turning the somewhat quiet state of Delaware upside down. Juice wasn't planning on letting the cops, Feds, or Hutch get a hold of him. He had already done ten years and wasn't planning on going back to jail let alone a Federal prison. He was feeling a lot better but still walked with a limp that was very noticeable. He stopped going in the 211 lounge because of how hot he was. If he was in Delaware he was in Claymont and Claymont only. Since the Feds were lurking around the neighborhood he decided to lay off of Hutch for awhile. He only came outside at night all of his clientele had to wait until nightfall to get their product from him. He wanted the Feds to have to work to get him, if they caught him.

Meanwhile Hutch had Riverside back the way it was when Starsky was still alive now that Juice was laying low.

"At least y'all hit that nigga I like the way y'all rode out that was definitely appreciated, you heard me?" Hutch said but wanted to know where Juice was hiding.

"Yeah but I want that nigga dead this waiting crap got me a little antsy." Baby Boy responded.

"I'm glad you letting us hustle out here with you now, that look out shit was boring but I want that nigga dead too so I put the word out to my boys that if they see that nigga and help me murk him they get a cut so now we have extra eyes." Shaheem added.

"Oh word." Hutch responded.

"Yeah and not just Riverside either if that nigga steps foot in this city somebody is going to spot him it shouldn't be hard he got a limp you should see him a mile away." Shaheem responded with laughter.

He was thinking that he should've hit something other than the back window while Juice was driving away. He knew if he was the one that killed Juice, Hutch would look out for him and he wanted that badder than he wanted Juice dead.

"That nigga drawing in the worst way possible I can't wait to put him in the dirt especially because he shot me." Baby Boy added.

"Yo let's go to the 211 lounge tonight I heard it be popping on Friday and Saturday nights." Shaheem suggested.

"Yo I don't go outside of Wilmington to party unless it's in Philly, I don't even consider Claymont as being part of Delaware." Hutch responded.

"Come on man just this one time if you don't like it don't go back but you need to relax and unwind a little bit you been tense lately old head plus I need to get out myself." Baby Boy added.

"Well since y'all dragging me to this bullshit all drinks are on y'all for the night and the door fee." Hutch responded hoping they would change their minds.

"We got you old head." Shaheem responded.

"Yeah we got you but you got to drink what we drink since we're paying." Baby Boy added.

"That's not a problem." Hutch responded.

A few hours later they pulled up to the parking lot. They could tell by the cars it was a nice crowd of people inside. Once they passed the bouncer there were girls everywhere. They were three of the few guys that were in there. Hutch threw his first shot of Patron back then Baby Boy brought him a double shot of Hennessy.

"Let me see you throw this back like you threw that Patron back." Baby Boy said.

"I'll take any shot y'all willing to pay for I come from a long line of alcoholics." Hutch responded with a chuckle.

"Say no more." Shaheem said as they started lining drinks up in front of Hutch.

"What's up man my name A I'm the owner I see y'all dudes buying out the bar." He spoke extending his hand to Hutch for him to shake it.

"I don't know you motherfucker. I'm only here because they wanted to come to this bullshit ass bar. I don't care if you're the owner and I ain't your mans so you can put your hand down." Hutch responded as he threw back another shot.

"When y'all finish these drinks right here y'all can get out my bar." A responded.

Hutch ignored that comment because he planned on leaving after those drinks were gone anyway. By the time Hutch got to his tenth shot he was ready to go. He wasn't the least bit entertained by the manager or the girls that were in there. Those drinks made him horny enough to have sex with ten girls that night but in no way was he drunk.

"I told y'all niggaz I come from a long line, I drank y'all youngens under the table give me the keys so I can take y'all home." Hutch laughed.

On their way out the door, the bouncer told them to have a good night. He liked the way Hutch handled his boss he never liked working for A. He thought of him as an arrogant spoiled little bitch.

"All right man you stay up." Hutch said as he nodded his head.

"I got to get to Sherelle house so I can burst one, them drinks got me feeling some type of way." Hutch thought to himself.

After he dropped Shaheem and Baby Boy off he headed straight to Chester to see Sherelle. When he walked in the door she was fast asleep. Hutch knew exactly how to wake his soon to be baby mom up. He slid off her panties from underneath her Teddy and helped himself to her clitoris. After a few sucks she woke right up.

"Damn, you know how to wake a woman up right don't you?" Sherelle asked.

"Yeah of course I do I had some black man Viagra at the bar so you know what you're in store for." Hutch responded.

They went at it until day break then they finally fell asleep. That was a night they'd both remember.

Meanwhile Juice was up at the crack of dawn working out trying to get back in shape since he lost a lot of weight when he got shot. He worked out during the day and hustled at night. He had plans to move to Baltimore after he reached fifty pounds. In three more months he did just that leaving Delaware with fifty pounds of weed and a half kilo of cocaine. He had ten thousand dollars to his name but knew that would change when he got to Baltimore.

CHAPTER TEN:

SANAA'S SECRET

It was Sunday night and Sanaa was ready to let her hair down. Xandu was having their usual Celebrity Sunday with Allen Ivan as the celebrity of the night. Women in the Tri-State area always flocked to an Allen Ivan party and the women always brought the guys out.

The club was so packed that they weren't letting anyone else in. Lucky for Sanaa she knew all the bouncers so they let her in. The people in line outside were angry but that's a part of the night life. In situations like that either you have to have major cash in your pocket to bribe the bouncer or you have to know someone at the door. In Sanaa's case she knew a lot of people in fact she made it her business to know who was a V.I.P in the Tri-State area.

There were guys dressed in their Evisu, Red Monkey, True Religion and every other name brand jean that were over expensive. As for the females they were dresses in True Religion, Antik, Salt and a lot of other expensive jeans. No one wanted to be out dressed at an Allen Ivan party. All with the exception of a hand full of people. It looked as if they were modeling for Platinum and Nieman Marcus stores in side of Xandu. The ballers were in V.I.P popping bottles of champagne as usual wanting Allen Ivan to know that they had money too.

Sanaa was having a good time like she always did at the club. If a guy popped a bottle of anything they poured some in her glass. She was just feeling like she made it to cloud nine when she spotted Bourbon walk pass the V.I.P.

"What the fuck is she doing here?" Sanaa thought to herself.

"I need to slow down on these drinks I'm following this bitch home tonight I see she by herself, bad mistake." She continued thinking.

For the rest of the night she kept a close eye on Bourbon. When Bourbon left she did the same. Sanaa followed Bourbon to some guy's house she was sleeping with. Bourbon didn't see Sanaa when she parked up the street behind her. Bourbon's late night lover didn't allow her to smoke marijuana in his house so she stayed outside to finishing smoking the rest of the Dutch Master she had burning.

Sanaa used that as an opportunity to sneak up on her after she saw that the car was full of smoke. She knew exactly what Bourbon was inside doing. She crept down the street to Bourbon's car and knocked on the window with her nine millimeter already cocked and ready to shoot.

When Bourbon looked up and saw who was knocking on the window she dropped the Dutch Master in her lap and it burned her inner thighs forcing her out of the car. When she opened the car door Sanaa grabbed her by her hair and dragged her out of the car.

"What the fuck?" Bourbon spoke.

But before she could finish her sentence Sanaa put the gun inside her mouth.

"So you think you can destroy my Benz, break in my apartment, steal my shit and break into my shop. Ransack that and thought you wouldn't be in the position you are in right now with me standing here with a gun in your mouth." Sanaa asked with an Are you serious? Look on her face.

Bourbon mumbled something but Sanaa wasn't trying to remove the gun to hear what it was.

"Well tonight you can tell Satan I said hello." Sanaa continued before she squeezed the trigger and left Bourbon's brains all over the pavement.

She ran off before anyone could witness what she had just done. She got in her car and drove off. It was the middle of the night so no one was up except Bourbon's late night lover who was in the shower at the time so she got away without any witnesses.

Bourbon's body wasn't discovered until someone came outside to go to work later that morning. When her late night lover came outside he found out why she never showed up after she called to say she was on her way there.

While the ambulance drove off with her body the police officers questioned everyone on the block to see if they heard or saw anything. When Sanaa finally made it home she went straight to the kitchen to pour herself a shot of Patron to calm her nerves. She never killed anyone before so her nerves were shot. After she took her fifth shot Tamia came into the kitchen.

"What's wrong S why are you killing that bottle like that?" Tamia asked.

"I'm not I just needed a few shots that's all." Sanaa responded.

"A few shots my ass that bottle was full I know because I brought it for you earlier today and you just came from the club so what's up?" Tamia asked in a more suspicious tone.

"Nothing I almost got into a fight at the club before it let out that blew my high I needed a few shots to calm me down that's all. Why are you acting all private eye on me?" Sanaa asked.

"I don't know S I mean I love you and if something is bothering you I want to know about it." Tamia responded.

"Well thanks for being so concerned I'm ok though I just want you to hold me tonight if that's possible?" Sanaa asked.

"That's not a problem, but it's tomorrow right now." Tamia responded.

"You play too much you know what I meant now let's go to bed." Sanaa responded.

"Okay come on." Tamia responded.

When they woke up Sanaa immediately turned on the news to see if any one saw her. When Tamia went to join her in front of the TV her mouth dropped when a picture of Bourbon came across the television. She couldn't believe it as the anchorman read the news.

A thirty year old Chester woman was found dead on Ninth and Butler Street around six o'clock this morning Divine Peterson was found by a man leaving for work earlier this morning. She was pronounced dead on arrival at Brozer Hospital we'll have more on the six o'clock news.

"She must have did somebody else dirty too, that's crazy I never would've thought that would happen, I just thought someone would beat the shit out of her for doing something shiesty to them but murder wow I'm fucked up over this." Tamia said while in a daze.

"Tamia." Sanaa shouted snapping her out of her daze.

"Huh." Tamia responded.

"Are you going to the funeral? I'll understand if you want to go I know that use to be your friend and everything but I will not be there." Sanaa said not really wanting her to say she was going.

"I might go to the viewing I don't really like funerals." Tamia responded.

"Okay well in that case I'll go with you I didn't want to go to the funeral for the people close to her to say something about me being there because they know we didn't get along. I just want to go to support you." Sanaa responded hoping she told her she didn't have to go.

"I know we had our little beef but I wouldn't wish death on anybody." Tamia said.

"Yeah me either." Sanaa agreed but deep down inside this was killing her.

Not telling her best friend and lover that she was the one that killed Bourbon.

Meanwhile 2Cent phoned Redds.

"Girl did you see the news this morning?" 2Cent asked.

"I ain't have to Bourbon's mom called me as soon as she found out I just been sitting here crying ever since." Redds responded.

"Damn I couldn't even cry I guess it'll hit me later I'm fucked up over this I don't know what to do with myself right now." 2Cent said.

"I wonder if Tamia saw the news." She thought to herself.

"Are you coming over here?" Redds asked.

"Yeah, as a matter of fact come get me so we can go over Bourbon's mom house." 2Cent responded.

"Okay I'll be there in an hour." Redds responded, needing time to get herself together.

Her eyes were blood shot red from crying uncontrollably.

"Damn, how could somebody do something like this nobody deserves that?" Redds thought to herself as she showered.

She got to 2Cent's house in an hour and a half. 2Cent usually would have said something smart about her not being on time but she left it alone. They rode in silence to Bourbon's mother house. When they got in front of the house they just sat there bracing themselves for what was in store for them once they got in there. After ten minutes they finally went inside.

"What the fuck took y'all bitches so long to get over here? Y'all her best friends, people she wasn't even close to made it over here before y'all." Bourbon's aunt wasted no time snapping on them as soon as they walked through the door.

"I needed some time alone before I came over here why you snapping on me for no reason." Redds shouted back.

"Look everybody all hostile and hurting but let's not take it out on each other." 2Cent jumped in.

"How are you doing Ms. Peterson? How are you holding up?" Redds asked.

"It's hard it's real hard losing your child you know." Ms Peterson responded as she rocked back and forth.

"If it's anything we can do just let us know." 2Cent added.

Before Ms. Peterson could answer Tamia walked through the door.

"I'm sorry for your loss Ms. Peterson if there's anything I can do just let me know here's my number." Tamia said.

"I know you didn't just have the nerve to walk up in my sister house like you was still cool with my niece." Bourbon's aunt started snapping immediately.

"Look I didn't come here for all of that I just came to give my condolences." Tamia responded trying to remain calm.

"Well we don't need your condolences, where your little girlfriend at I know she somewhere enjoying this shit." Her aunt continued to argue.

"Any way Ms. Peterson you have my number if you don't feel the same way your sister does call me if you need anything." Tamia said as she turned her attention back to Ms. Peterson ignoring her sister's comments.

"Tamia wait I'll walk you outside." 2Cent said.

"Yeah hold up." Redds added.

"Look ,you know how Macy is don't let that get to you, but what I really wanted to say is I apologize for anything I had to do with this beef between us and your girlfriend. We were better than that it shouldn't have gone that far." 2Cent said once they were outside hoping for forgiveness.

"Me too I apologize for my part in that also." Redds added.

"I except y'all apology but Sanaa is the one y'all should be apologizing to I mean y'all did start it when y'all wrecked her car that was fucked up I had her under control when I pulled her away from y'all inside the club." Tamia responded.

"Yeah we know we will when we see her I just hope she don't start her shit up." Redds said thinking about Sanaa's attitude problem.

"If I'm there when y'all do it I'll make sure she don't, but I'll see y'all at the viewing I can't go to the funeral I don't want to have to fight Macy I do have respect for my elders and with my temper I'm going to snap if she keeps running her mouth." Tamia responded.

"I know what you mean we almost got into it a couple of times." 2Cent responded.

"All right y'all keep y'all heads up I'll holla at y'all." Tamia said as she got in her Escalade and pulled off.

"I ain't think she was going to come down here I was wondering if she saw it on the news earlier." 2Cent said.

"I didn't think so either I thought she was going to just go to the funeral." Redds added.

"You want to go smoke before we go back in there because you know Macy is going to be nosey wanting to know what we were talking to Tamia about and she hype too. You know how she is when she's like that." 2Cent said convincing Redds that they needed to smoke.

"Yeah let's go get a Dutch." Redds answered.

As soon as they got in the car Macy started shouting out the door to them.

"And where do y'all bitches think y'all going at?" Macy yelled.

"We going to the store we'll be right back." Redds yelled back.

"Well, bring me a Pepsi." Macy ordered.

"Girl that's why I need to smoke I can't deal with her right now I hate when she have these mood swings." 2Cent stated as they pulled off.

When Tamia got back in the house, Sanaa was sitting on the couch with the television off sitting in silence.

"Why is it so quiet in here? Are you all right?" Tamia asked.

"I'm just thinking that's all I know your taking this kind of hard so I was trying to think of a way to take your mind off of things for a while." Sanaa responded.

"All I want you to do is be there for me I just came from Bourbon's mom house and her aunt snapped on me, but Redds and 2Cent were there too they apologized for their behavior during the feud between them and us but I told them they need to apologize to you. So if you see them at least hear them out and don't snap just to squash this shit once and for all." Tamia asked trying to reason with Sanaa.

"Okay, for you I'll accept the apology but I think they should replace everything they took from me and our shop if they really want to squash it." Sanaa replied.

"Let's get the apology out the way first, before we get to all of that." Tamia responded relieved she didn't snap on her for going to see Bourbon's mother in the first place.

"I'm going out to get some air Mia I'll be back do you want something from the store or anything?" Sanaa asked.

"No, I'm okay I got everything I need right here, except what's about to walk out that door." Tamia said with a smile on her face.

"So you need me?" Sanaa asked with a big grin on her face.

"Of course I do now hurry up back." Tamia responded.

"Tamia knows the right thing to say at the right time, all the time I am really blessed to have her, but I can't tell her I killed Bourbon I already feel bad for doing it." Sanaa thought to herself.

She rode around for an hour before she decided to get some ice cream so Tamia wouldn't question her when she went back in the house. Killing Bourbon was far from easy on her conscience it ate away at her even after the funeral. Sanaa wasn't the same after that night she drank more than usual. Even though she could relax because they had no witnesses or leads, she stopped going out to the club, she wasn't talking so much at the shop.

Tamia noticed the change in her behavior but didn't ask about it. She just tried to cheer her up by taking her to Hibachi's one of her favorite restaurants. She brought Sanaa a whole new wardrobe and increased the quality time she spent with her. They went to the Laff House on South Street, Warm Daddy's, Temptation's and after all of that Sanaa still didn't snap out of the deep depression she was in.

Tamia ran out of ideas until she finally got fed up and started trying to talk to Sanaa to see what was bothering her.

"What's wrong S? You haven't been yourself lately. I've been patient and tried to cheer you up but all I get is half of a smile. I want my baby back you been acting like this since Bourbon got killed. It's like you took it harder than I did and I'm the one that used to be cool with her so do you want to talk about it?" Tamia asked hoping to get an answer besides the usual nothing Sanaa's been giving her lately.

Sanaa sat silent for about ten minutes before she finally spoke.

"Mia I don't want to tell you because I don't know how you're going to react or if you're going to look at me different or not. It's been killing me too because you're the only one that I can confide in and at the same time the less you know the better, if the outcome isn't good but I did something really bad." Sanaa said hoping she wouldn't have to actually say it.

"What, what did you do?" Tamia asked.

"It has something to do with when I started acting how I have been lately." Sanaa said giving Tamia a hint.

"You don't have to say it and I won't look at you different but I understand why you did it so relax a little bit." Tamia said trying to comfort her.

"You're not mad?" Sanaa asked.

"No I love you Sanaa." Tamia said hoping her words would sooth Sanaa.

"I love you too Tamia can you hold me?" Sanaa asked.

"I don't see why not." Tamia responded.

A month later Sanaa was back to normal laughing and joking a lot more than she did before the murder. She even started going back out. When she pulled up in front of Cavanaugh's she was showing off the new Aston Martin That Tamia brought her. She got her status in the club back in no time.

While she was there she met a party promoter and he showed her the ropes of party promoting. She felt good knowing she could finally bring something to the table to help Tamia with her Fashion Show for her clothing line. She thought about throwing an after party for it and everything.

Sanaa finally started feeling like a burden was lifted off of her. When she got in from the club she immediately started telling Tamia about the party promoter she met and the idea she had about and after party. To Tamia, Sanaa was a new person and she liked it.

CHAPTER ELEVEN:

GAME OVER

It's been a year since Bourbon died and Tamia was almost completely out of the game. It's been six months since Juice migrated to Baltimore. He left with fifty pounds of marijuana and was on his way back up to the Tri-State area for a hundred more.

Tamia was on her last two trash bags and she was completely out of the drug business forever. She couldn't wait to be done all of her drawings for her clothing line was complete.

The first Fashion Show was scheduled to go on after she sold the rest of the marijuana she had in her possession. Everything was back to normal finally, after the chaos. She was on her way to meet Juice at the half way point in Delaware.

"Don't blame Spazz cause I ain't invent the game I just rolled the dice trying to get some change and I'll do it twice ain't no sense in me lying as if I am indifferent man." Singing along with Jay-Z but twisting the words up a little.

"One more trip from Juice and I'm officially done I know Hutch will be calling real soon so he'll finish this last bit off." Tamia thought to herself. At the rate she was traveling her and Juice would be pulling up at the same time.

"I can't believe I made ten million dollars from hustling this is the shit you only read about or see in the movies I did it real big on the low." Tamia thought to herself.

She felt like she accomplished something and she did but she still had a battle ahead of her. She could sell drugs to people but could she sell clothes to them, that they would want to wear? That remained to be seen. Juice was pulling up just as she was.

"What's up Juice how you been?" Tamia asked.

"I've been good how about you, you got any more after this or I have to start looking for a new Connect today." Juice asked letting her know he was upset she was leaving the game.

He looked but couldn't find another Connect with Marijuana as good as hers but he had too much pride to tell her that.

"Look I got like a hundred and fifty pounds left I got enough for your re up if you're grabbing another hundred. The other fifty is somebody else's but if you grab the whole one fifty in a couple of days they're yours." Tamia responded.

"I might can get all of it but hold that hundred for me definitely." Juice responded.

She actually had one hundred seventy five pounds left but didn't want to tell him that because she planned on keeping twenty five pounds for herself. She hadn't smoked marijuana in a while because she didn't believe in smoking and selling at the same time.

The way she saw it she had some time to make up for. Tamia had enough for her and Sanaa to smoke for the rest of their lives. She didn't allow Sanaa to smoke either while she was selling.

"Okay guess I'll see you in a few days." Tamia responded as she pulled off.

Juice already had his plan mapped out in his head. He had enough dope sells and marijuana sells waiting for him when he got back to Baltimore to have enough money to buy all one hundred and fifty pounds. He didn't want to be without any marijuana because that was his top seller he was new to the city so the fiends weren't going to him as quick.

Although he had clientele, that clientele was mostly weight. When Tamia got back to Chester she went to go count the money after she made sure it was exactly sixty five thousand dollars. She started bagging what she had left which took the rest of the night realizing she miss calculated. She actually had two hundred and thirty pounds left.

"Good I can hit Juice off with one hundred and fifty, Hutch with fifty and I can keep the other thirty for me and Sanaa and I'm done." She thought to herself.

She started packing up everything so she could take a nap before she had to go to the shop. Her cell phone rang as soon as she was finished.

"What's up Hutch?" Tamia answered.

"I need them Spazz ASAP." He responded.

All right I'm on my way give me twenty minutes." Tamia said.

"Damn I can't even get any sleep I'm glad I'm about to be done with this shit soon." Tamia thought to herself. As soon as she got to Interstate 495 her phone rang.

"Every day I'm hustling." rang through the speakers.

"Yizzo." Tamia answered.

"Yo I'm coming to get them baby girl the whole buck fifty." Juice said.

"What the fuck that quick?" Tamia snapped.

"Yeah I was up all night grinding, on top of that I had money waiting I got it popping out here you heard me?" Juice responded, feeling proud of him self.

"All right man I'll see you there." Tamia responded.

"Finally I'm done with this shit." She said to herself as she pulled up around the corner from Riverside.

"What's up Hutch this is it baby boy I'm done after this I got one more drop to make and I'm done I'm out for good. It was nice doing business with you for so many years and to show how much I appreciated your business, I only need half the money for these fifty pounds good luck on finding another connect and be careful out here the game is changing and it's for the worst stay up, and I hope to see you when you get out the game." Tamia said as she gave him a big hug.

"Thanks that's good looking girl." Hutch responded as he started counting out the money to Tamia.

"Thanks it was a pleasure and I found a new connect the other day but his weed ain't as good as yours is though, good luck Spazz." Hutch said as he headed to his car.

Tamia went back to Chester to get the hundred and fifty pounds then headed to Baltimore to meet Juice. On her way back she thought of Sanaa and the reaction she was going to have about her staying out all night but it was worth it now she can concentrate on her clothing line.

When Tamia walked in the shop Sanaa immediately stopped doing her client's hair and pulled Tamia in to the office.

"I wonder what that's about." Keisha whispered.

"Yeah me too." Amber whispered back. Once the door closed Sanaa started yelling.

"Where the fuck you been at all Night and it better be the hell good?" Sanaa snapped demanding an answer.

"Look it's a surprise can it wait until we get home. I'm already behind on my appointments. I want to get caught up but in the mean time I wasn't with any one if that's what you were thinking. I was finishing up some business now can we go back out there and take care of those clients out there?" Tamia asked hoping she would forget about it for now.

"Okay but we are not done talking about this shit" Sanaa responded.

All eyes were on them when they walked out of the office. Everyone in the shop heard their conversation because of how loud Sanaa was. As for the ones that heard the rumors but weren't sure if they were true or not. It was confirmed right then and there that Tamia and Sanaa were an item.

"What y'all looking at? Acting like y'all never heard an argument before." Sanaa snapped. Everyone went back to doing what they were doing before Tamia walked in.

"So how's the clothing line coming along Tamia?" Keisha asked in an attempt to loosen the tension.

"Oh it's coming along fine I'm almost done with the drawings for it." Tamia responded.

"Okay I can't wait to show off my hairstyles I made some up especially for the fashion show." Keisha said with a Kool Aid smile on her face.

"I can't wait either I know that's going to get my clientele up sky high with all of that publicity." Amber added.

"Yeah we might have to expand and open another shop we have enough clientele coming in here as it is." Sanaa said adding to the conversation.

When Sanaa turned her back Tamia mouthed the words thank you to Keisha. Keisha then mouthed the words your welcome back to Tamia before Sanaa could turn back around to catch them.

For the first time in years Tamia's phone was actually silent the whole time they were in the shop. When Sanaa picked up on it she said something about it.

"What no hotline today, Mia? That's a first." Sanaa said being her sarcastic self.

"Yeah I know. no one loves me today I guess." Tamia responded picking up on the sarcasm. Sanaa called Tamia's phone when she wasn't looking.

"Shorty like mine, baby that's why I'm addicted to how we kick it and everything you say to me." Bow Wow came through her speakers but Tamia ignored it.

"You are such a smart ass I guess you thought you didn't have a special ring tone." Tamia said as she shot Sanaa a look.

"Ooh that's my ringtone? I feel special now." Sanaa responded smiling like a little girl who was told she was pretty.

"Yeah that's your ringtone and I guess you love me today huh?" Tamia responded.

"Yeah I love you even though I'm mad at you." Sanaa responded moving her head from side to side.

"You won't be mad when you find out what the surprise is." Tamia responded rolling her eyes playfully.

"We'll see about that, all finished." Sanaa responded to Tamia and spoke to her client at the same time.

Fifteen minutes later Tamia was done her last client. Keisha and

Amber finished their last clients a half hour afterwards. They cleaned up before they locked up and left the shop. Tamia and Sanaa followed each other home. When they got there Tamia pulled out a trash bag a quarter of the way full. Sanaa immediately became suspicious.

"What's that?" Sanaa asked.

"Well it's a lifetime supply of weed for the both of us that's what I've been trying to tell you, I'm officially out the game that's why my phone haven't been ringing all day, that's why I was out all night one of my major clients moved to Baltimore. He grabbed a hundred pounds then when I got back last night I bagged everything that I had and it took the rest of the night, and as soon as I was about to come home to take a nap my Delaware dude called and then that nigga down Baltimore called me right back. So after I took care of them I grabbed the last thirty pounds that I was keeping for us and came to the shop." Tamia explained. Sanaa made a squealing noise.

"Mia you're done you're finally done, I hope you got a bottle to celebrate." Sanaa said as she gave Tamia a hug.

"Yeah I got one upstairs if you didn't drink it last night without me." Tamia said with a raised eyebrow.

"Don't look at me like that I drank some Patron I didn't drink it." Sanaa responded with an innocent look on her face as they walked upstairs to their apartment.

Once inside Sanaa went straight to the kitchen to pour two glasses of Moet. When she went back into the living room Tamia was rolling a Dutch Master for them to smoke. Sanaa gave Tamia a glass and made the toast.

"Game over?" Sanaa said raising her glass. Tamia clanged glasses with Sanaa

"Game over." Tamia responded. They finished the bottle then lit the Dutch up.

"You know weed makes me horny right?" Tamia asked already buzzed.

"Yeah me too." Sanaa said as she rubbed on her thigh.

"You don't want to wait until this Dutch is finished?" Tamia asked. Sanaa moved closer to Tamia's ear.

"No let's play a game, let's play keep the Dutch lit while we play with each other and who ever let it go out has to go down on the other person for an hour and a half." She whispered.

Tamia's eyes almost popped out of her head as she said okay. They started to touch and smoke at the same time passing the Dutch back and forth as one licked and sucked all over each other taking turns until it was gone.

"I guess we both win." Tamia said with a smirk on her face.

"Yeah so I guess we'll have to roll another one." Sanaa said with a smirk on her face.

"What? I'm already high are you serious?" Tamia asked.

"Yup that way someone has to lose, we're both high as a kite I'll roll up this time let your hair down and have some fun." Sanaa responded.

"Okay, go right ahead and roll up." Tamia responded.

She knew as high as she was she was going to let it burn out. She didn't have the energy to go down on Sanaa for an hour and a half. While Sanaa rolled, Tamia came up with a plan she was going to play puff puff give with Sanaa, knowing she was going to hold the Dutch longer than two puffs. Sanaa lit the Dutch and started smoking. Tamia counted six puffs before Sanaa passed the Dutch. Tamia held it for a few moments while Sanaa was too busy sucking away at her breast to realize she was letting it burn. Tamia took two puffs before she passed it back. Before you know it Sanaa had let the Dutch burn out. Tamia was happy her plan worked in her favor.

"Looks like you lost the game the Dutch is out and you're holding it." Tamia said with a smirk on her face.

"Yeah looks like but you're going to lose the next time." Sanaa responded as she spread her legs and helped herself to her vagina. They fell fast asleep after two hours.

"So did you sleep good last night?" Tamia asked as soon as Sanaa started to awake from her slumber.

"Yeah did you sleep good, I know you had to have several orgasms during that hour and a half last night. All nice and high I had fun though what about you?" Sanaa asked.

"Of course I had fun but we're going to have more nights like last night and maybe some better now that I have a lot more free time on my hands." Tamia responded.

"So when are we going to look at a house Mia?" Sanaa asked.

"As soon as you want we can start tomorrow if you want." Tamia responded.

"You know we are going to be in the shop all day tomorrow how about Sunday and Monday?" Sanaa asked.

"Okay Sunday or Monday it is but you can call Century 21 to set up an appointment with an agent though." Tamia responded.

"Oh it's done and so is the shopping for the furniture wait until you see what I got your going to love it." Sanaa responded.

"I bet I will." Tamia responded. Sanaa stepped into the bathroom to shower. Tamia's phone rang unexpectedly.

"Yizzo." She answered.

"Yo Spazz I was thinking since you aren't in the game anymore would you be able to turn me on to your connect?" Juice asked going out on a limb.

Since he couldn't find a new connect he knew he'd be out of weed soon. He was the only one in Baltimore with marijuana that good and he wanted to keep it that way.

"Nigga you know damn well I'm not going to do that. He way the fuck in New York it ain't like he in Philly and besides he told me day one he don't want to meet any one." Tamia snapped.

"But I can't find another connect down here. I'm the only one with work like this down here. what do you want me to do I got it popping down here, you good so you don't care about nobody else eating my man said you was a thorough chick." Juice said out of anger.

"Hold the fuck up who you think you talking to pussy you don't be screaming at me like I'm your fucking daughter. For one and for two you act like you my peoples or something that was strictly business off the strength of our mutual friend and what the fuck I look like the Good

Samaritan of the fucking year. You Better take that bullshit to somebody else you don't know who you fucking with." Tamia responded as she hung up in his ear.

"That motherfucker got some nerve. Who the fuck he think I am he must don't know he can meet face to face with Satan for talking to me like that ooh he got me steaming." Tamia mumbled to herself.

"Who was that Tamia?" Sanaa asked after she walked out of the bathroom.

"Just some dumb nigga I use to sell weed to asking me to turn him on to my connect babe is he serious?" Tamia asked letting off some steam. Sanaa started to undress Tamia.

"No baby he can't be serious nobody would do that unless it was someone they were cool with boo. But let me relieve some of that tension for you he got my baby all worked up." Sanaa said as she started giving her a massage. Before they knew it they lost track of time. Sanaa's phone rang.

"Hello" Sanaa answered.

"Umm are y'all on y'all way because there is a line out here and we were supposed to be open like forty five minutes ago?" Amber asked.

"Oh yeah we're running a little late we'll be there shortly okay." Sanaa said gesturing Tamia to get in the shower.

"Okay well how long are y'all going to be so I can tell these people something before they get any more pist off." Amber responded.

"Give us twenty minutes." Sanaa responded as she lied about how long they were going to be.

They were going to be at least another half hour to forty five minutes. As soon as Sanaa hung up the phone, one of her clients called.

"I am so sorry Ms. Ruth I woke up late I'm on my way I'll be there shortly." Sanaa said without even saying hello.

"Well I am hungry do I have time to go get something to eat and come back?" Ms. Ruth one of her elderly customers asked.

"Sure if you're going to Burger King or McDonalds you don't have time for B&C's or John Doggies I won't be that long." Sanaa responded.

"Well okay I'm starving so I'm kind of glad you're running late." Ms. Ruth responded.

Tamia came out of the bathroom as soon as she hung up the phone and rushed to iron her clothes. By the time Sanaa got finished taking another shower Tamia was already dressed and ironing something for Sanaa to wear.

"Now how you know I wanted to wear that?" Sanaa asked trying to catch an attitude.

"Look come on we're late just put it on you look fly in it I get horny every time I see you in it." Tamia responded. She had to throw Sanaa a curve ball so she wouldn't argue.

"Okay well since you put it that way I'll wear it." Sanaa said with a smile on her face.

"Thank you." Tamia thought to herself.

They got to the shop a half an hour later and the crowd outside was unbelievable.

"And you wanted to play a little while longer with all of this work we have to do." Tamia said cutting her eye at Sanaa before they got out of the Escalade.

Now that Tamia stopped selling drugs she had the time to take walk in customers and appointments. Even though she had a little over ten million Tamia had big dreams she needed every dollar she could make. It took them until eight o'clock to get rid of the crowd that was outside when they pulled up.

"Can I make a suggestion?" Keisha asked.

"Sure go ahead." Tamia responded.

"How about you two give one of us or both of us a set of keys to the shop so we can get in and start doing hair if y'all happen to run late again because that's putting us all behind schedule by letting the line build up. If we could've got a few heads out before y'all got here and took more people that wanted to walk in and made some more money." Keisha explained.

"That's a great idea." Sanaa responded cutting her eye at Tamia.

"That way I can play with you in the morning for as long as I like or until one of our first appointments." Sanaa thought to herself.

"Yeah okay that is a good idea I see you're hungry I'll make both of you a set of keys tomorrow." Tamia responded.

"I just don't have to give y'all a key to the office or the supply closet everything y'all need is out here besides I take inventory and stock the shelves every night anyway so it wouldn't be a problem." Tamia thought to herself. Keona came in and interrupted her thoughts.

"Mia I know I don't have an appointment but can I get a quick weave put in plus I got some news that you might want to hear." Keona asked hoping she said yes.

"Yeah I got time go sit at the sink so I can wash your hair I'll be there in a minute." Tamia responded. She got a towel and headed over to where Keona was.

"So what do you have to tell me?" Tamia asked.

"Girl, Bourbon brother Shawn supposed to come home next month. I don't know what he did to get his sentence reduced but yeah, he get out next month and word is he coming straight here. So watch your back when you leaving out of here at night." Keona responded.

"Good looking out I'll have a police escort at night when I leave here that ain't about nothing." Tamia responded nonchalantly.

"Oh okay that's good thinking." Keona responded.

After the shop closed, and Keisha and Amber left, Tamia told Sanaa the news.

"I need another gun." Sanaa thought to herself.

"Look we going to have a police escort from now on. I don't want anything to happen to you and I know you're going to flip out if anything happens to me. So I think this is best and we should move before he gets out that way no one knows where we live." Tamia gave her opinion.

"Okay Mia it seems like you have everything all figured out if that's how you want to handle it okay." Sanaa responded not putting up an argument.

"But I'm still getting another gun just in case." Sanaa thought to herself.

They went home and had another sexcapade. The next morning Tamia's phone rang.

"Hello." Tamia said hesitantly because she knew even though Sanaa's eyes were closed she wasn't really sleep.

"So how are you?" The voice said on the other end.

"I'm fine and who is this?" Tamia asked not catching the voice.

"You just stopped calling did I turn you off or something?" Ice asked.

"Uh, no you didn't turn me off it's just that I had just met you and didn't feel the need to explain. But since you're asking me to, I'm bi sexual and my girlfriend told me she wanted me all to herself so I ended us before we even got started. But if you want to get technical you didn't pick up the phone either." Tamia responded after she picked up on the voice.

"Oh, that was unexpected, well can I meet the person that's keeping you away from me is that too much to ask?" Ice asked hoping she said yes.

"Well how about I ask her and call you back in a few she's still asleep." Tamia responded.

"Okay, but I want to take you two to dinner at Moshulu on Sunday." Ice responded.

"That sounds nice if I get the okay." Tamia responded.

"Okay well call me back with an answer then I'll make reservations." Ice said before he hung up.

"Who was that?" Sanaa asked after Tamia pushed end call on her cell phone.

"I knew you weren't sleep that was Ice he said he wanted to meet you and he wants to take us to dinner at Moshulu on Sunday. But I don't know if you want to go then we'll go but if you don't then we won't. I'm leaving it up to you I don't want you to feel uncomfortable about the situation." Tamia responded.

"So you're leaving it up to me huh?" Sanaa asked.

"Yeah." Tamia responded.

"Well I don't see the harm in it you forgot to tell him exactly how jealous I am though." Sanaa replied.

"All right I'll call him back are you sure?" Tamia asked.

"Yeah,unless you have something to hide." Sanaa said insisting that they went on their date with Ice.

As the week went by Tamia couldn't believe how anxious Sanaa was about Sunday. But when Sunday finally came, anxious turned to nervous.

"Are you sure you're up for this S I mean you seem a little nervous?" Tamia asked.

"Yeah I'm up for this." Sanaa responded.

"So are you ready to go or do you need a few more minutes?" Tamia asked a little uneasy about the situation.

"Yeah I'm ready let me finish putting on my make up." Sanaa responded. After fifteen minutes they headed to Philly.

"Look Sanaa when we get up here please do not make a scene I have to tell you like a little kid." Tamia said not wanting to be the center of attention as usual after Sanaa flipped out.

"Oh so I'm a little kid now you taking your daughter to meet your new boyfriend?" Sanaa asked sarcastically.

"See you starting already not right now Sanaa I was making a statement you getting all bent out of shape for nothing." Tamia responded.

"I don't think it's for nothing." Sanaa said not wanting to leave the conversation alone.

"Look just drop it we are trying to go and have a good time tonight." Tamia said sternly.

"Yeah we are because if he's as cute as you say he is we are going to have some fun tonight." Sanaa responded.

"I know you are not thinking what I think you're thinking matter of fact I don't want to know." Tamia responded as she turned the radio up.

They rode listening to the radio for the rest of the ride to Philly. When they pulled up lucky for them they had a place to park it was so packed. When they walked up Ice was waiting by the door.

"Hello lovely ladies how are you two this evening?" Ice asked.

"I'm fine how about your self?" Tamia responded.

"I'm okay now that tonight finally got here." He responded.

"That's good well Ice this is Sanaa and Sanaa this is Ice." Tamia said as she gave the introduction.

"Well hello it's so nice to finally meet you." Ice said with a comforting smile.

"Hello." Sanaa responded.

"Let's go eat shall we?" Ice said before they went inside.

"You girls can order whatever you like on the menu. You don't have to take it easy on my pockets." Ice said wanting them to know he had money.

"Oh we were, because if you can't pay for whatever we order we surely can." Sanaa responded.

"I knew she wasn't going to behave herself." Tamia thought to herself.

"Well is that right? Don't worry I'm holding." Ice responded.

"That's so nice to know." Sanaa replied feeling the need to get the last word.

"So, Ice how's business going? The last time we spoke you said you had a car lot?" Tamia asked playing referee.

"Business is great I opened up another one actually, how's the Shop?" Ice asked.

"The shop is doing fine Sanaa here is my partner actually." Tamia responded.

"Yes I am her partner in every way you could imagine." Sanaa interrupted wanting to rub that in Ice's face.

"Well Ice, Are you still building houses or are you just doing the car lot thing?" Tamia interrupted trying to keep the piece.

"I'm still doing both I'm renting out a few apartments now also." Ice responded.

"So tell me, how long have you two known each other?" Ice asked continuing the conversation.

"Since we were twelve, Mia and I have been tight since the day we met always having each other's back opened a salon now here we are." Sanaa answered.

"Yeah and we are thinking about expanding starting a chain of salons one salon at a time." Tamia added.

"So you're not going to tell him about the clothing line Mia?" Sanaa asked.

"Well you just did Sanaa." Tamia responded.

"I'm intrigued if it's okay with the both of you can we all be friends the three of us?" Ice asked not seeing the harm in all three of them hanging out every once in a while.

"Sure we can all be friends as a matter of fact why don't you show us where you live after dinner." Sanaa suggested.

"Are you sure this is a good idea you know how jealous you get Sanaa?" Tamia responded.

"Yeah I'm sure if it's okay with you?" Sanaa asked.

"I'm fine with it if you are." Tamia responded.

After they ate the girls followed Ice to his Condo down the street.

"Wow I didn't know he had a Condo on Delaware Ave." Tamia said.

"Now I'm impressed." Sanaa added.

"I wonder how he decorated the inside." Tamia said.

"Me too that's why I suggested he show us where he lived so I can be nosey." Sanaa responded looking at Tamia with a sly look on her face.

"You never cease to amaze me sweetheart never." Tamia said shaking her head from side to side.

"Well he's waiting let's go inside." Sanaa responded.

They got out of the car and walked over to the door.

"Well are you ladies surprised we didn't have far to go?" Ice asked.

"Yes." The girls said in unison.

"Well let's go up I'm on the seventh floor." Ice suggested.

"Lucky number seven huh?" Tamia said flirting a little.

"Yup, lucky number seven." Ice responded as they got off the elevator.

"This is me seventy ten ladies first." Ice said as he opened the door and turned on the lights.

"Wow this is nice." Sanaa said.

"Yeah it is." Tamia agreed.

"So who was your interior decorator or did you decorate yourself?" Tamia asked.

"I did it myself why do you ask." Ice responded.

"This is very impressive I never met a man with this much taste before." Tamia responded.

"So are you going to show us the whole Condo? Wow you even have a view of the Delaware River." Sanaa asked as she discovered the patio.

Ice gave them a tour starting with the kitchen and ending with the bedroom.

"I love King Size beds." Tamia said.

"So do I." Sanaa agreed as she grabbed her hand and escorted her over to the bed.

"It's just enough room for us to roll around in." Sanaa added. Ice's eyes almost popped out of his head when the words left Sanaa's mouth.

"Ooh and it's soft." Sanaa said as she bounced up and down on it.

"Yeah it is soft." Tamia agreed.

"Just like you." Sanaa said seductively before she leaned in and kissed Tamia. In a matter of seconds they were giving Ice a show he'd never forget.

"Are you going to stand there and watch with your tool all hard or are you going to join us?" Sanaa asked seductively.

"Since you put it like that how can I resist." Ice responded as he started to undress trying not to reveal just how excited he really was.

"Let's help him undress." Sanaa suggested. When the girls started to help, Ice almost had an orgasm in his underwear.

"You girls sure do know how to make a man feel like a king." Ice said as he closed his eyes and relaxed.

"Oh yeah you're going to really feel like a king in a minute." Sanaa responded as she reached in her purse and pulled out a pair of handcuffs.

"What are you about to do with those?" Ice asked a little frightened.

"You are enjoying yourself aren't you?" Sanaa asked.

"Yeah." Ice responded.

"Well these are going to boost your enjoyment a little. I'm going to handcuff you to the bed and we are going to play with you and each other while you are cuffed. I want to tease you a little it'll drive you crazy not being able to touch us I promise." Sanaa responded trying to get Ice comfortable with the idea.

"Okay I'll play along." Ice responded a little more at ease.

Sanaa handcuffed his right wrist to the head board then cuffed the left leaving Ice totally helpless except for the use of his legs.

"This isn't comfortable for me I'm feeling handicapped right now. Ice said looking at his wrist handcuffed.

"You're about to be in ecstasy in a minute." Sanaa responded.

"Where the fuck did this bitch get handcuffs from I never seen her with handcuffs and two pair at that." Tamia thought to herself as she watched Sanaa take charge.

Tamia decided to join in the fun as she started to kiss Ice slowly on his chest. Ice was enjoying every minute of it as she worked her way down.

"Oh, she looks like she's enjoying this a little too much." Sanaa thought to herself as she joined in the fun.

After Ice had his orgasm he was so relaxed he didn't notice Sanaa going over to her purse. When she got there she pulled out a .22 caliber pistol and some tape before he could open his eyes Sanaa taped his mouth and cocked the pistol.

"What the fuck?" Tamia said startled when she came out of the bathroom.

Ice opened his eyes once the tape was on his mouth. He struggled to get loose to no avail when he saw the pistol pointed at his head.

"So you want to take my baby away from me huh? This is my pussy and you can't have it." Sanaa said.

"What the fuck are you doing Sanaa? You heard me tell him I was with you. That's why I couldn't see him you agreed to meeting him. I told you this wasn't a good idea you fucking tripping put the gun away and let's go." Tamia said hysterical.

"This is to make sure he doesn't come between us just in case you change your mind." Sanaa responded.

"Look Sanaa if you trying to prove to me how much you love me, look I got the picture a long time ago. I never cheated on you and never thought about cheating on you. I'm yours please just put the gun down you don't have to do this." Tamia pleaded with her.

"Yes I do have to do this Mia, he still wants to be in the picture that's not a good thing. When you know I'm jealous, not only do you know I'm jealous, but you also told him I'm jealous but he didn't listen he had to invite both of us to dinner." Sanaa said then turned her attention back to Ice.

"I know what you were thinking but your three some ended in a fatal way goodbye Ice." Sanaa said as she grabbed a pillow, put it over his face and squeezed the trigger.

Tamia just stood there in shock looking at ice's limp body and Sanaa standing there with the gun in her hand.

"Come on wipe off everything you touched including him we got to get the fuck out of here you done lost your mind." Tamia said coming out of her shock.

After they cleaned off their finger prints they left the apartment rushing down the stairs and out the door. On their way to the car Sanaa shot the desk clerk and took the surveillance tape out before she got in the car. Tamia headed for the highway still not believing how Sanaa just transformed in front of her eyes.

When they made it home Tamia's body went numb from what she had just witnessed. Somehow she got herself stuck in a world wind of triangles in which a few of them ended up fatal. One triangle she wasn't even aware of, the beef between Hutch and Juice being both of their marijuana connection.

Everything finally caught up to Tamia and it put her in a daze and nothing was going to bring her out of her state of mind not even Sanaa. Morning came when they heard an unexpected knock at the door.

TO BE CONTINUED.

REST IN PEACE

Family
LELIA BRANDON – GRAND MOTHER
ALLEN BRANDON – UNCLE
MARY FARMER – GREAT AUNT
BETTY FARMER – GREAT AUNT
SARAH WILLIS - AUNT
PETE SMITH – GRAND FATHER
ELSIE MAY HARDING – GRAND MOTHER
ROBERT HARDING – UNCLE
LEONARD "PEACHES" HARDING - UNCLE
MELVIN HARDING – GREAT UNCLE
NATHAN DAVIS SR. – UNCLE

Friends & Associates

KARIM ALEXANDER
RICHARD "SALEEM" SALTERS

HENRY "ICE" RAMEY
NATALIE NICOLE MCCREADY
BRIAN "BOOG" DICKERSON
JANIRA "SUGAR" RICHARDSON
MARLON D. JOHNSON
ARTHUR B. FRANKLIN III
KHALI "STACKS" HENSON
JESSIE SHAW
DARREN D. MAJEED

COMING SOON

TRI-STATE TRIANGLE part 2
2011 Female calendar
2011 Male calendar
For the grown & sexy
For updates
Email me @: tamikad.harding@yahoo.com
Or
Myspace me @: www.myspace.com/Tamika_D_Harding
FaceBook me @:
Facebook.com/ Tamika D. Harding
Or write:
Tamika D. Harding
Hu$tle With Fine$$e
P.O. Box 81
Chester, PA 19016

TO ORDER ON LINE

Log On To
WWW.HustleWithFiness.com
Or
WWW.HustleWithFinesse.biz